Interior of Cave 4

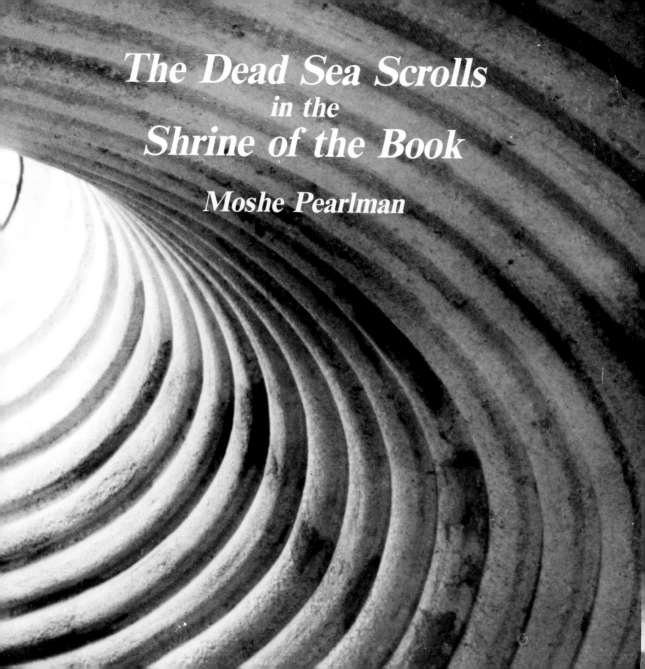

The Dead Sea Scrolls
in the
Shrine of the Book

Moshe Pearlman

The Israel Museum, Jerusalem

Design: Ora Yafeh
Photo editor: Irene Lewitt
Consultant: Magen Broshi
Production: Batya Segal

Photographs: Sandu Mendrea (cover),
Helen Bieberkraut, Werner Braun,
Moshe Caine, David Harris, Edi Hirshbain,
Rolf Kneller, Kodansha Publishers,
Garo Nalbandian, Ronald Sheridan

Color Separations: Scanli Ltd., Tel Aviv
Plates and Printing: Kal Press, Tel Aviv

ISBN 965-278-007-3
Sixth edition 1999

Contents

Author's Note:
Part of the text in this book
is based on my *Digging up the Bible*,
by kind permission of the publishers,
Weidenfeld and Nicolson, London.
M.P.

Foreword

This book, which is meant to serve as an introduction to the Shrine of the Book, is also a concise layman's guide to the Dead Sea Scrolls and related material.

The Scrolls, which came to light exactly forty years ago in Qumran, constitute the most important archaeological find ever made in the Holy Land or, for that matter, anywhere in the world. The accidental discovery of the Scrolls marked the beginning of an era of stupendous discoveries. Once established, the possibility of unearthing manuscripts in the Judaean Desert led to a frantic search for other caches. And indeed, following the sensational finds at Qumran, additional manuscripts were uncovered at half a dozen sites, enriching us with documents of diverse types, as well as various periods – from the time of Alexander the Great to the Middle Ages. The new discoveries had a tremendous impact on scholarship and promoted a myriad of publications. However, part of the manuscripts remain unpublished, and an international team is still at work preparing a comprehensive analysis. It is hoped that in ten years' time, this rich material on the Scrolls will be available in its entirety to both scholars and laymen.

The Shrine of the Book fills the need for a general survey of the Dead Sea Scrolls. We were fortunate in having Mr. Moshe Pearlman agree to prepare such a text. Mr. Pearlman, alas, did not live to see his lucid and illuminating book in print. This versatile man, who had distinguished himself as a soldier, civil servant, and prolific author, died on April 4, 1986, and is sorely missed by us all.

Located at the Israel Museum, the Shrine of the Book, the D. Samuel and Jean H. Gottesman Center for Biblical Manuscripts, is the most popular tourist attraction in Jerusalem with the exception of the Wailing Wall. Its fascination derives not only from its unique contents, but also from its remarkable architectural conception. Designed by the American architects Fredrick Kiesler and Armand Bartos and opened to the public in 1965, the Shrine of the Book has become one of Jerusalem's outstanding landmarks.

Martin Weyl
Director, The Israel Museum, Jerusalem

View of Qumran and the Dead Sea

The Discovery

The Discovery

The Shrine of the Book in Jerusalem's Israel Museum offers a unique encounter with history. Housed in a structure that is itself an architectural gem are priceless treasures, among the rarest in the world. They are ancient writings of immeasurable scholarly value, excavated or acquired under unusual circumstances by Israeli archaeologists in our own generation.

The most spectacular are eight Dead Sea scrolls of leather, well preserved after being hidden for nineteen hundred years in pottery jars in the dry atmosphere of below-sea-level caves. Following meticulous decipherment and study, they proved to be the most sensational documentary discovery of the century, shedding light on the history, life and thought of ancient times, on the Hebrew Bible (the Old Testament) and the Talmud, on Hebrew and other early languages, and on the influences that helped shape the development of Christianity in its opening decades.

Thousands of manuscript fragments have been recovered in the Dead Sea area in the last few years; but on display in the Shrine of the Book are rare leather scrolls that are complete or of substantial length.

The building was erected specially to house these precious documents, though it soon became the natural setting for other ancient writings discovered during archaeological excavations in the country. The most notable of these are the documentary treasures yielded by the exploration of the Bar Kochba caves near the Dead Sea, and they appear together with the artefacts found at the site and the "action" photographs which capture the hazards of the expeditions.

The story of the Shrine and its exhibits may be said to have begun on 23 November 1947, with an urgent telephone call to Professor Elazar L. Sukenik, who held the chair of archaeology at Jerusalem's Hebrew University. The call was from a friend, an Armenian dealer in antiquities, living in the walled Old City of Jerusalem. He needed to see the professor on a matter too sensitive for the telephone, and he requested an early meeting.

This was not easy, for Palestine was then in turmoil. The United Nations General Assembly was considering a resolution — due to be adopted any day — to partition the country into two independent states, one Jewish, one Arab, upon the termination of the British Mandate. And the Arabs were threatening to attack Jewish cities and villages throughout the land if it were carried.

Letters of the Hebrew alphabet from 1st century C.E. ossuary inscriptions (left) and the War Scroll (right)

In the city of Jerusalem with its mixed population, the British authorities had erected security barriers, and a military pass was required to get from one zone to the other. The professor was on one side and the Armenian on the other. Neither could secure a pass quickly. They accordingly arranged to meet next morning at the barrier between the two sectors.

At this odd meeting place, talking to each other across the narrow "no-man's land" of hooped barbed wire, the Armenian told a strange tale. He had been visited the previous day by a fellow antiquities dealer, an Arab from Bethlehem, who had brought him a few pieces of leather on which there appeared to be some kind of old writing. The Bethlehemite said he had got them from some Bedouin who claimed they were parts of leather rolls they had found in a cave near the Dead Sea, and he sought the Armenian's appraisal. The Armenian had now come to the expert, Professor Sukenik, for his opinion, and if they were really parts of authentic ancient documents, and valuable, perhaps the professor would care to buy them for the Hebrew University.

He then pulled from his pocket a scrap of parchment which he held up for Sukenik to see, and the professor peered through the loops of barbed wire trying to make out the writing. The script looked familiar, very much like the Hebrew writing he had seen scratched or carved on stone tombs belonging to the 1st century that he himself had discovered in and around Jerusalem. But he had never seen such inscriptions written in ink on leather. And for a very good reason: stone endured; leather was perishable. Nevertheless, he had a hunch that this piece of leather was genuine — "the real thing", as he wrote later in his journal. However, he could not be sure until he could examine it carefully, and perhaps be given the opportunity of studying the complete scroll. He therefore urged his friend to go to Bethlehem as quickly as possible and bring back, if not the scroll, at least additional samples. He in the meantime would secure passes to be able to get to the Armenian's store at a moment's notice. Sukenik's excitement at the prospect of studying these documents is readily understandable when one considers the profound importance of a body of ancient writings to our knowledge of history. Where no written records exist, the clues to a bygone age are usually to be found in the remains studied by archaeologists — buildings, fortifications, weapons, tools, domestic utensils,

The Discovery

water installations, altars, temples. From these clues the scholar tries to reconstruct the human story of the peoples in antiquity — how they fought, hunted, farmed, worshipped, died. Writings, however, are far more than clues. They are clear communications from the past, the direct utterances of the ancients, speaking to us of their lives and thoughts and codes of conduct, and relating their chronicles. How much more significant are such writings when found in the Holy Land, belonging perhaps to biblical or immediately post-biblical times, and supplementing, possibly illuminating further, what we already know from the Scriptures. Small wonder that Sukenik waited impatiently for a message from his Armenian friend.

It came in a telephone call on 27 November. The Armenian had obtained more pieces of "the leathers", and they were in his store. The professor hurried over. Careful scrutiny convinced him that they were indeed fragments of genuine ancient Hebrew manuscripts, and he was ready to go with his friend to Bethlehem to negotiate for the purchase of the complete scroll.

In the tense conditions then prevailing, for a Jew to travel in an Arab bus through Arab-populated territory even for the few miles from Jerusalem to Bethlehem was a most hazardous undertaking. Sukenik's family thought him impetuous and irresponsible, and were adamantly against his going. He therefore spent the next day, 28 November, utterly frustrated, sick at the thought that the scrolls, only a short distance away, were just beyond his reach. However, the radio that evening carried the news that the U.N. decision on Palestine had again been postponed, and would be put to the vote the following night. The professor then remembered something his son Yigael had told him which pointed to opportunity. (Yigael at the time was Chief of Operations of Haganah, the Jewish underground defence force, and Yadin was his code-name. He adopted it as his family name when the State of Israel was established in May 1948.) Yadin had said that widespread Arab attacks were expected *after* the U.N. vote. That, thought Sukenik — as he wrote later — gave him a whole day for a final effort to secure the scrolls.

Slipping out of the house shortly after dawn, and armed with his pass, he crossed the British barrier, woke up his Armenian friend, and they were soon on the bus to Bethlehem, which they reached without incident. A few minutes later they were closeted with the Arab antiquities dealer.

Dead Sea Scroll fragment shown to the late Prof. Sukenik. It proved to be part of the Thanksgiving Scroll.

The Discovery

For Sukenik's benefit, the dealer repeated the story told him by the Bedouin. They belonged to the Ta'amira tribe and had been moving with their goats along the northwestern shore of the Dead Sea when one of the flock strayed. They clambered after it but it was soon lost to view. Noticing the opening to a cave where the animal might be sheltering, they cast stones through the entrance. The responding sound seemed to be that of stone hitting pottery, and they crawled into the cave to investigate. There they found several sealed earthenware jars which, when opened, were seen to contain bundles of leather covered by a strange kind of writing. Thinking that perhaps someone might consider them worth a little money, the Bedouin had kept them as they continued with their flocks through the Judaean desert until their next visit to Bethlehem, the market town of the area, and had come to the antiquities dealer for his advice.

The dealer now brought out for Sukenik's inspection three jars, and carefully drew forth the scrolls. The professor gently unrolled one and began to examine it. It was with deep emotion, as he later wrote in his journal, that he glanced at the opening sentences and was astonished at being able to read and recognize the beautiful biblical Hebrew script. It gave him the feeling that he had been "privileged by destiny to gaze upon a Hebrew scroll that had not been read for more than two thousand years". (Quotations from his journal are taken from extracts that appear in "The Message of the Scrolls" by Yigael Yadin. The account of the acquisition of the scrolls is also based on this book.)

He had little doubt that the scrolls were indeed authentic and not a clever forgery, but he had to be absolutely certain. He therefore told the dealer that he would probably buy them, but would wish to study them further under more suitable conditions, and would give his reply within forty-eight hours. The dealer agreed, and Sukenik walked out of the store with the scrolls wrapped in newspaper. There were uneasy moments when he and the Armenian, the only ones in western dress, took their place in the bus queue, and a group of Arabs began moving towards them with angry gestures and threatening shouts. Fortunately the bus arrived in time and they were able to board it without being molested. They reached Jerusalem and alighted at the Old City's Jaffa Gate, Sukenik crossing back into the Jewish zone with his treasure.

A page of Prof. Sukenik's diary "I read a little more in the 'skins' . . . We may have here one of the greatest finds of this country, a discovery we have never dreamed of."

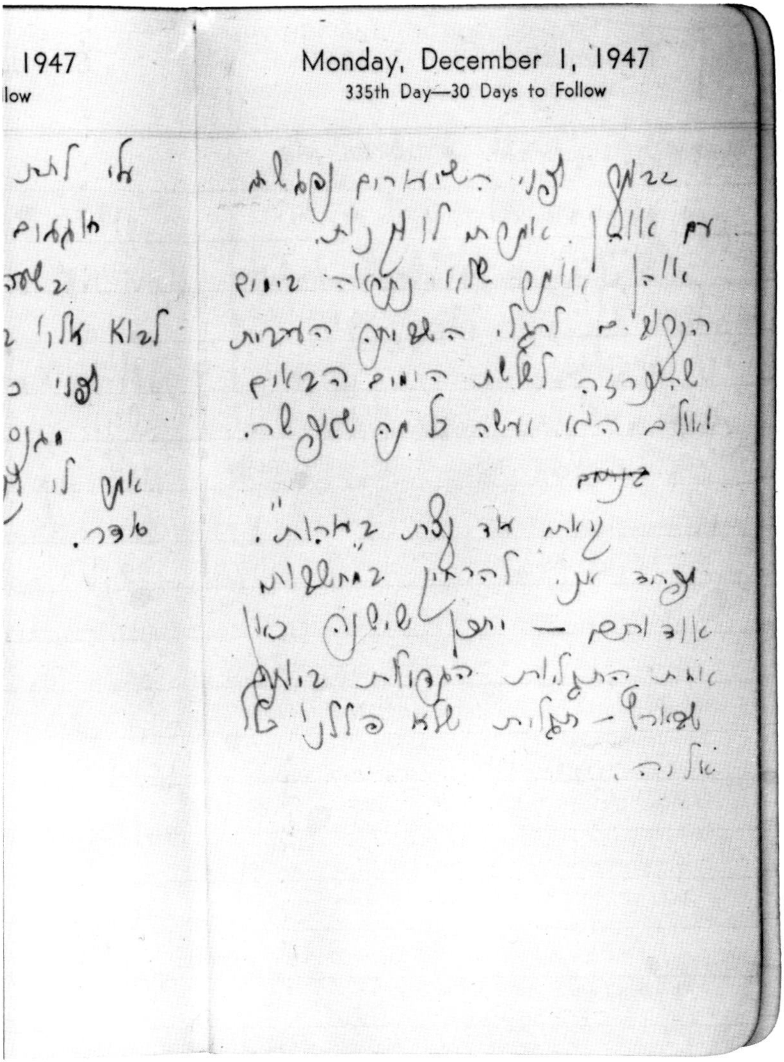

1947
llow

Monday, December 1, 1947
335th Day—30 Days to Follow

בבוקר לפני השיעורים נפגשתי
עם אורן. אמרתי לו מה נלך.
אורן אומר שהוא שמח ביום
הקשה להיות השמחה החיצונית
שהכריזה לעשות היום הבאים
ועלם היה ורשה כל כך שמחה.

~~ביום~~

יוצאת אל "עבודת במחלקת".
עובר אני להראות במחשבות
אחד רגש — והוא ששמחת כמו
אותה התגלות העממית בזמן
שמחה — תגלית שלא פללתי
אליה.

The Discovery

Back at home, Sukenik went straight to his study and began examining the scrolls. And he was still engrossed in this absorbing work several hours later when the family rushed in to tell him what they had just heard on the radio about the U.N. Assembly meeting: the Palestine Partition resolution had been carried. There was to be a Jewish state. "This great event in Jewish history," Sukenik wrote in his journal, "was thus combined in my home in Jerusalem with another event, no less historic, the one political, the other cultural."

The following morning he telephonéd the Armenian to say he was buying the three scrolls for the Hebrew University, and despite the dangers — Arab attacks had broken out immediately — they managed to meet, and the purchase price was handed over.

One of the scrolls turned out to be the biblical Book of the prophet Isaiah, and contained more than half the text of this work. (Fragments of additional chapters were discovered later.) It was Sukenik's opinion, subsequently confirmed, that this document was about one thousand years older than the earliest copies previously known of the traditional Hebrew text. (One was the Codex of the Prophets, copied by Moses Ben Asher in 895 C.E., and preserved in a Cairo synagogue; the other, from the synagogue of the Sephardic Jews in Aleppo, Syria, was a manuscript of the whole Bible, dating back to 929 C.E.) The implications of this find for biblical scholarship were to be of enormous importance.

The remaining scrolls were to have a similar impact on other areas of scholarly studies. One was a prophetic account in biblical Hebrew of a war of destiny in which good would ultimately triumph over evil. It was described as The War of the Sons of Light against the Sons of Darkness. The second scroll was a collection of Hebrew verses resembling, at first glance, the Book of Psalms and is now known as the Thanksgiving Scroll.

Sukenik's erudite detection and brief preliminary study had thus launched the research, which will engage scholars for many years to come, on the most famous manuscripts in the world, the Dead Sea Scrolls.

But this was only the beginning of the adventures which eventually were to bring all the complete parchment scrolls to the Shrine of the Book.

The Aleppo Codex,
Proverbs 5:18 – 6:31
Ben Zvi Institute Collection MS1,
on loan to the Israel Museum

עינו דכות עינו ה̇ ועיניו תחלינה ולא כחד ויבזיח אבשלום ולעשות הטוב יחה מעל את עינו תראינה יראו עינו כוין קרץ בעינו ׃

יהי מקורך ברוך ושמח מאשת נעורך
אילת אהבים ויעלת חן דדיה ירוך בכל
עת באהבתה תשגה תמיד ולמה
תשגה בני בזרה ותחבק חק נכריה
כי נכח עיני יהוה דרכי איש וכל
מעגלתיו מפלס עוונתיו ילכדנו
את הרשע ובחבלי חטאתו יתמך
הוא ימות באין מוסר וברב אולתו ישגה

בני אם ערבת לרעך תקעת לזר כפיך
נוקשת באמרי פיך נלכדת באמרי פיך
עשה זאת אפוא בני והנצל כי באת
בכף רעך לך התרפס ורהב רעיך
אל תתן שנה לעיניך ותנומה לעפעפיך
הנצל כצבי מיד וכצפור מיד יקוש

לך אל נמלה עצל ראה דרכיה וחכם
אשר אין לה קצין שטר ומשל
תכין בקיץ לחמה אגרה בקציר מאכלה
עד מתי עצל תשכב מתי תקום
משנתך מעט שנות מעט תנומות
מעט חבק ידים לשכב ובא
כמהלך ראשך ומחסרך כאיש מגן

אדם בליעל איש און הולך עקשות פה
קרץ בעינו מלל ברגלו מרה באצבעתיו
תהפכות בלבו חרש רע בכל עת
מדנים ישלח על כן פתאם יבוא אידו

שנא ה̇ כי כל תועבת יהוה אשר שנא ולא תקים לך כי שנא אבשלום
כי שנא אלה שש הנה שנא יהוה ׃

ראשך ב̇ ובא כמהלך ובא מתהלך ׃ ירמיה ראשך תנינה רישך כל ׃
ואל תטש ואל תטש גרגרתך כתב ׃ חסר ואמות גרגרותך כתב ושארא
גרגרתיך ׃

פתע ישבר ואין מרפא
שש הנה שנא יהוה ושבע תועבות
נפשו עינים רמות לשון שקר
וידים שפכות דם נקי לב חרש
מחשבות און רגלים ממהרות לרוץ
לרעה יפיח כזבים עד שקר
ומשלח מדנים בין אחים

נצר בני מצות אביך ואל תטש
תורת אמך קשרם על לבך תמיד
ענדם על גרגרתך בהתהלכך
תנחה אתך בשכבך תשמר עליך
והקיצות היא תשיחך כי נר מצוה
ותורה אור ודרך חיים תוכחות מוסר
לשמרך מאשת רע מחלקת לשון
נכריה אל תחמד יפיה בלבבך
ואל תקחך בעפעפיה כי בעד
אשה זונה עד ככר לחם ואשת
איש נפש יקרה תצוד

היחתה איש אש בחיקו ובגדיו
לא תשרפנה אם יהלך איש
על הגחלים ורגליו לא תכוינה
כן הבא אל אשת רעהו לא ינקה
כל הנגע בה לא יבוזו לגנב כי
יגנוב למלא נפשו כי ירעב
ונמצא ישלם שבעתים את כל הון

ובגדיו ל̇ וקדש הוא ובגדיו את ראשו לא יפרע ובגדיו יקרעו
ואדמה וייחתו איש ׃

The Discovery

Shortly after he had acquired the first three, Sukenik learned of the existence of another four scrolls. (The eighth was acquired only in 1967.) At the end of January 1948, he received a letter from a Jerusalem Arab who, like the Armenian, sought a meeting to get the professor's expert judgement on some Hebrew parchments he had in his possession. The Arab belonged to the Syrian Orthodox Christian community, and was an emissary of the head of his church, Mar (Bishop) Athanasius Samuel, known as the Syrian Christian Metropolitan, of the Monastery of St. Mark in the Old City of Jerusalem.

After complicated arrangements they met in the Arab sector. The emissary showed him four scrolls, explaining that they had been bought from a Bedouin of that same Ta'amira tribe, and adding a story of their discovery similar to the one Sukenik had heard from the Bethlehem dealer. He now asked if the professor would be interested in buying them. Sukenik noticed that they were similar to the first three scrolls, and when he unrolled part of one, he saw immediately that it was another biblical manuscript of Isaiah. He told the emissary that he would wish to take them home for further study, and would give him an answer the following week.

Sukenik spent day and night examining the new scrolls, and judged that their origin was the same as that of the other three, and that they too were about two thousand years old. He was particularly taken by the Isaiah scroll, finding it in better condition that the one in his possession. Moreover, this one contained all the sixty-six chapters.

Sukenik arrived with the scrolls for the next meeting with the emissary on 6 February 1948 ready to purchase them for the Hebrew University and asking the price. But upon hearing that the professor was sufficiently interested to buy, the emissary made transparent excuses, saying he could not name the figure as he needed time to think it over, and he took back his scrolls. They made a tentative appointment to meet one week later which the emissary was to confirm. He never did, and that was the last Sukenik saw of these four scrolls. He died in 1953 in the sad belief that they were lost to his people. He could never have imagined that they would be retrieved by his son a year later.

Prof. Sukenik studying the Thanksgiving Scroll

The Discovery

It transpired that the emissary had been sent by his bishop to elicit from Sukenik an opinion on the antiquity and value of the scrolls. It was the bishop who had acquired them several months earlier in the manner the emissary had described. He had shown them to a few scholars but they had failed to recognize their significance, dismissing them as not more than three hundred years old. Some time later he heard from members of his congregation that Professor Sukenik had purchased similar scrolls. It was then that he had sent his man to the professor with a fictitious offer to sell, and Sukenik's excitement when he saw the scrolls told the bishop's representative all he wanted to know: they were indeed writings of great antiquity and very valuable.

Mar Athanasius Samuel had been advised by American friends that he would get a much higher price in the United States. They had also urged him to get the documents out of the country quickly as Palestine, already torn by violence, was likely to be ravaged by full-scale war between Arabs and Jews when the British Mandate ended in May.

Thus, there was no "next meeting" at which Sukenik expected to buy the scrolls. Instead they were taken out of the danger zone in March, and ten months later were brought to America by the bishop himself, who hoped to sell them for a reported sum of several million dollars. Soon after his arrival, he was urged to allow the publication of facsimiles of the documents, as this would both make available source material for research, and also stimulate interest among potential buyers, such as wealthy scholarly foundations or institutes of higher learning. He agreed, and facsimiles of three scrolls were accordingly published by the American School of Oriental Research, edited by Professor Millar Burrows of Yale's Divinity School, in 1950 and 1951. The scrolls themselves, however, remained in a vault, unsold; and for the next five years bishop Samuel continued his fruitless endeavours to dispose of his precious documents.

The turn in his fortunes came in 1954. In that year Sukenik's son, Yigael Yadin, was on a brief visit to the United States. He had been chief of staff of the Israel Army from 1949 to 1952, and had then left the service to resume his archaeological studies. For scholarly as well as for sentimental reasons, he had been completing preparations for the publication of a book on the three scrolls

Artificial caves near Qumran, including Cave 4, the richest of the caves

The Discovery

on which his father had been engaged until his death. He had then spent a year studying and writing a comprehensive commentary on one of them, The War of the Sons of Light against the Sons of Darkness, and had been invited to lecture on his work at American universities. One morning he received a telephone call from a friend telling him of an advertisement in the Wall Street Journal that would surely interest him. Yadin got the newspaper and found, sandwiched between business notices, a small paragraph which read: "The Four Dead Sea Scrolls: Biblical Manuscripts... for sale ... an ideal gift to an educational or religious institution." A post box number followed.

Yadin had little doubt that these were the very scrolls his father had seen and had expected to buy from the bishop's emissary. He had learned at the beginning of his U.S. visit that the bishop had been unable to sell them, had blamed the advisers who had urged him to allow publication of facsimiles of three of them, and had therefore refused to allow publication of the fourth. He now wished to sell all four as a package. Yadin had also heard that the asking price had dropped considerably from the original millions.

Yadin was unwilling to reply himself to the box number in the advertisement, fearing possible leaks which might prompt Arab agents to prevent the sale to an Israeli. He therefore acted through an intermediary, and after speedy negotiations with a representative of the bishop, the deal was concluded for $250,000. Securing a bank loan for this amount required collateral or a government guarantee. Yadin cabled Jerusalem and received a prompt reply: "Prime Minister and Finance Minister delighted with wonderful opportunity. Order for suitable guarantee dispatched. Mazal-tov."

One month after he had placed the advertisement, the bishop himself, Mar Athanasius Samuel, accompanied by his aides, met with Yadin's representative in New York's Waldorf Astoria Hotel. The scrolls were in the hotel vault. They were checked, found to be authentic, removed, handed over against payment, and were on their way to Israel the following day.

The major part of the cost was later contributed by New York industrialist and benefactor Samuel Gottesman. When he died, his children established in memory of their parents the Shrine of the Book as a centre of biblical and scroll

Wall Street Journal advertisement that led to the purchase of the Dead Sea Scrolls

THE WALL STREET JOURNAL.

Copyright, 1954, by Dow Jones & Company, Inc.

. CXLIII. NO. 105 ★★   NEW YORK, TUESDAY, JUNE 1, 1954   Entered as Second Class Matter at the Post Office, New York, N. Y.   10 CENTS in and

YORK AREA

ellent labor sup-
the U. S. Em-

ill consider
lant and giv-
free rent.

information write
Wall Street Journal

Equipment
ip Available

rofit Opportunity
gnized as tops in
field.

n capital required.
select and train
int and supervise
tural, and mate-
aler organization.
s as to business
ancial ability. All
nfidential.

Wall Street Journal
t., Chicago 90, Ill.

LE
AND OFFICE
NED 2nd COMM.

ay St., Balto., Md.,

2,500 Tb. capacity
Heating furnished
Near B. & O. Ter-
and new Wash-
ediate possession.
ing to responsible

REAMER, Atty.
itable Building
re 2, Maryland
e: LE 9-5454.

U WISH TO
R SELL
SINESS

Size—Anywhere
UCH WITH

RET CORP.
Business Brokers
St., Brooklyn
-5600

TELS

ale a large group
rts in varying

---

sold through above or related chan-
nels. Plant equipped with latest
automatic machine tools. Aggres-
sive sales organization. Basis for
working relationship open. Inquiries
invited from responsible parties
Write: President.

Box F-32
The Wall Street Journal

SMALL ESTABLISHED MANUFACTURER DESIRES SALES REPRESENTATION

We sell to glass companies and
some plumbing houses. Entire
U. S. available except New York
and Penna. Will consider nation-
wide set-up or breaking it down
into areas. Write fully concerning your operation and expected
conditions to:

Box F-81
The Wall Street Journal

Southern manufacturer with Gross
Sales of $1,000,000 per year needs
$125,000 working capital. Will give
ten year first mortgage at 6%
interest on plant and equipment ap-
praised at $300,000. Plant is in the
center of one of the country's lead-
ing industrial cities and consists of
seven acres and 70,000 sq. ft. of
floor space. Approximately half of
the floor space is leased for ten
years to reputable tenant for approximately $12,000 per year
Box F-112, The Wall Street Journal

FOR SALE — PROFITABLE BUSI-
NESS. INDUSTRIAL CRATING,
WOODEN BOXES, ETC. LOCATED
IN VIRGINIA.
ON ACCOUNT OF OWNER'S
HEALTH, MUST SELL NOW
REPLY BOX E 202
THE WALL STREET JOURNAL

MACHINERY & EQUIPMENT

FOR SALE LORAIN CRANE

T. L. 20, ½ yd.

MISCELLANEOUS FOR SALE

"The Four Dead Sea Scrolls"

Biblical Manuscripts dating
back to at least 200 BC, are
for sale. This would be an
ideal gift to an educational or
religious institution by an in-
dividual or group.

Box F 206, The Wall Street
Journal.

10,000-18,000 gal. STEEL TANKS,
2 electric WELDERS, 2 ALIG.
SHEARS, 1 ECONOMY BALER;
new 2" SOIL PIPE; 1 DIESEL
LOCO. CRANE. In Ind., Ohio, Va.,
Ill.

H. GREENBERG
Murphysboro, Illinois

REAL ESTATE SALE RENT—LEASE

Approximately 40,000 Sq. Ft. at $1.85
per Sq. Ft. All accommodations of
heavy industrial zone. Bringing approximately 25% annually. Call
SHerwood 2-3700. Mr. Orlando C.
Ruggiero.

FOR RENT OR LEASE

FOR RENT KNOXVILLE, TENN.

Recently remodeled brick building. Three blocks from main

FOR RENT OR LEASE

Summer rental in New Jersey, com-
pletely private ranch cottage, 1½
hours from New York, secluded 5
room modern cottage, spring water,
blazing riding trails through pine
woods, private pond. $800 per
month.
Box F-185, The Wall Street Journal

Ideal for broker or local office out-
state corporation. 600 feet Ave. of
Americas at 57th St. Hotel connec-
tion. $2400. CH. 4-4628.

REAL ESTATE FOR SALE

YACHT WORKS
Long Established Business Located Northern Coast Of New Jersey.

Fully Equipped:

Carpenter Shop
Woodworking Shop
Paint Shop
Machine Shop

Large Inside and Outside Storage
Facilities.
Complete Parts Inventory.
Cruiser Slips, With Walks, Elec-
tricity and Running Water.
Owner Retiring.

FOR SALE

The Discovery

research, named The D. Samuel and Jeane H. Gottesman Center for Biblical
Manuscripts. The four scrolls would now join the three already in Israel, so that
the country would be in possession of the seven best preserved Dead Sea
leather scrolls then known to be in existence. An extensive eighth scroll
would be acquired by Yadin in 1967, and would also be housed in the Shrine of
the Book.

One of the four newly purchased scrolls, as we have seen, was another
manuscript of the Book of Isaiah. The second was the Habakkuk Commentary,
an interpretation of the words of the prophet and their application to events of
the 1st century B.C.E. The third was The Manual of Discipline, a detailed code of
conduct written by the original owners of the scrolls. These three manuscripts
were in Hebrew, and had appeared in facsimile in America. The fourth, which
had not yet been published, but would be studied and issued later in Israel, was
in Aramaic. It turned out to be a literary work elaborating on dramatic episodes
in the opening Book of the Bible and is now known as The Genesis Apocryphon.

View of Qumran, the marl plateau
and the rocky cliffs

The Sect and the Scrolls

The Qumran Sect

The scrolls were part of the library of a small, ascetic and devout Jewish sect who gave their own rigid interpretation of the laws and injunctions in the Five Books of Moses, and who were bitterly critical of the Jewish religious establishment in Jerusalem, charging the Temple priests with being lax and corrupt.

At an early stage in that history, during the latter half of the 2nd century B.C.E., its members, apparently seeking a deserted spot where they could isolate themselves and live a strictly disciplined and collective way of life, had gone to dwell at the site now called Qumran on the northwestern shore of the Dead Sea. The site was abandoned after an earthquake in the time of Herod towards the end of the following century, but was soon resettled by the same sect, whom most scholars now identify with the Essenes. According to Flavius Josephus, the 1st century C.E. Jewish historian, the Essenes were celibates who lived in a monastic group. They did not marry, they owned no private property: everything belonged to the community. The Essenes believed that the priests in Jerusalem were not the legitimate priests, that the Temple was not built according to the correct specifications and that the laws of purity and impurity were not sufficiently strict. The Essenes continued to live in Qumran in accordance with their rigid views and rules right up to 68 C.E., when the site was destroyed by the Romans. That was the third year of the five-year war of the Jews against the legions of Rome which ended in Roman victory.

It was during the two hundred years of their occupancy of Qumran, the turbulent final centuries of the Second Temple period, that this Dead Sea community copied books of the Hebrew Bible — which had been written several centuries earlier — as well as other Jewish writings, and also composed and copied their own sectarian literature and codes. When it had seemed likely that they would be overwhelmed by the Roman army, the Essenes hid their sacred works in the almost inaccessible caves in the nearby cliffs to save them from the hands of the conquering infidels. There, some of them wrapped in linen and sealed in tall pottery jars, the scrolls had remained untouched until their dramatic discovery in 1947.

Pottery vessels found in the Qumran pantry

With the extraordinary impact of these scrolls on biblical, historical, theological, paleographic, linguistic and literary scholarship, the search began for the site of the sect, and the ruins of Qumran were brought to light during archaeological excavations in 1951 and 1953–56. They were conducted jointly by Dominican Father Roland de Vaux, Director of the French Biblical and Archaeological School in Jerusalem, and Gerald Lankester Harding, Director of Jordan's Department of Antiquities in Amman. (Before the 1967 Six-Day War, Qumran was under Jordanian control.)

They found the remains of the communal buildings and installations of this Dead Sea sect. These included the scriptorium; a large assembly hall which also served as the communal refectory; grain silos; flour mills; a kitchen and bakery; a forge; and workshops, the most impressive of which was an uncommonly well-preserved pottery factory, complete with a plaster platform for kneading the clay, and two kilns. The scholars also discovered the elaborate water system of the community, with pools and plaster-lined cisterns which were fed by flash-floods channelled by aqueduct from Wadi Qumran. Here, then, were the installations necessary for the independent subsistence of an isolated desert commune. For protection there was a fortified tower. The members' living quarters were tents, huts and nearby caves.

The scriptorium discovered by the archaeologists is of special interest, for it was in this writing room that they found the very tables used by the Qumran scribes when copying the biblical scrolls and inscribing the sectarian works. The main table, made of plastered clay, was sixteen and a half feet long and one and a half feet high. Nearby were the remains of two shorter tables. In the debris of this room De Vaux also found two inkpots, one of bronze and the other of terra-cotta. One of them still held traces of dried ink made of lampblack and gum.

The archaeologists also found coins. Among them were a group of copper coins belonging to the latter part of the 2nd century B.C.E., an additional clue which helped date the beginnings of the Qumran community settlement. Also found were coins belonging to the second and third year of the five-year war of the Jews against the Romans (66 to 70 C.E.). These were recovered from a layer of ashes caused by the Roman destruction.

The Qumran Sect

The numerous pottery fragments found in the ruins are exactly the same type as that of the pottery jars in which several of the Dead Sea scrolls had been sealed. This direct link between Qumran and the manuscripts was further proof that the antiquity of the scrolls could not be later than 68 C.E., when the Roman legions conquered the site, and was almost certainly earlier.

There was nothing in the excavations to indicate with certainty whether the community fled their settlement with the approach of the Romans, or whether they put up a fight and were slaughtered. Whichever it was, writes Frank Moore Cross Jr. in a piquant comment in his "The Ancient Library of Qumran and Modern Biblical Studies", they "were prevented from carrying away their manuscripts, with the result that their library, abandoned in nearby caves, survived. Ironically, had the community survived, the manuscripts no doubt would have perished".

The cave in which the first group of seven Dead Sea Scrolls were discovered in 1947 is located about three-quarters of a mile to the north of the Qumran site. It is now known as Qumran Cave 1, for its discovery stimulated further search in the Qumran area by both Bedouin and archaeologists for additional caves containing documents, and with each success, the new cave was numbered according to the chronological order of its discovery. Five were found in 1952. In one of them, Cave 3, there was the find of a unique copper scroll (at present in the Archaeological Museum of Amman), listing, describing and giving the locations of hidden treasures, possibly real, but probably imaginary. Another, Cave 4, south of Cave 1 and much closer to the Qumran ruins, held considerable portions of scrolls and thousands of manuscript fragments. Parchment documents were discovered in four other caves in 1955. And early in 1956, additional scrolls were found in an eleventh cave about half a mile north of Cave 1. The most impressive finds were those in Caves 1, 4 and 11, with the best preserved manuscripts in Caves 1 and 11. Those caves were further away from the Qumran settlement, and may possibly have been pre-selected as safe hiding places when danger from the Romans appeared imminent. What is certain is that the scrolls had been secreted with care — two pottery jars in Cave 1 in which two of the linen-wrapped scrolls had been sealed were still unbroken.

Map of the Dead Sea and the Judean Desert where the scrolls and other documents were discovered

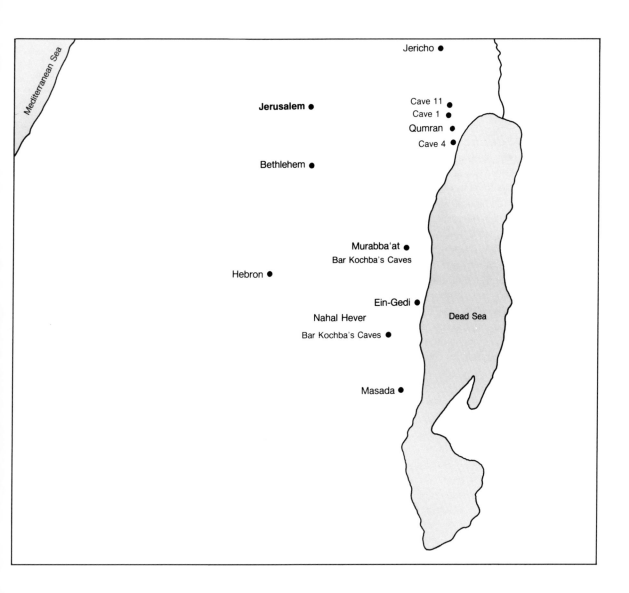

The Qumran Sect

Cave 4, on the other hand, held the largest quantity of writings, comprising the bulk of the books in the Qumran library. Many had disintegrated over the centuries into thousands of fragments. However, after painstaking work of identification and reassembly, many of them have also proved of considerable scholarly value.

The total yield of all eleven caves in the Qumran area are manuscripts of almost seven hundred works, biblical and sectarian. They range from complete scrolls to fragments with only a few sentences. Many are copies of versions of the same work. The texts of books of the Hebrew Bible number more than one hundred and seventy, and each biblical book, with the sole exception of the Book of Esther, is represented in these Dead Sea documents. The biblical books with the largest number of copies found in the caves were those of the Pentateuch (the Torah), with seventy, and Psalms, with twenty-seven. Of the Pentateuch — the Five Books of Moses which form the holiest section of the Bible for Jews to this day — the list was headed by Deuteronomy. Isaiah topped the list of copies of the prophetic works.

Thus, although the Cave 1 scrolls, the first to be discovered, may be said to have provided the revolutionary basis of modern scroll research, the documentary material discovered later in the other ten Qumran caves has vastly expanded that research, and shed brighter light on the fields of scholarship associated with these ancient writings.

Central showcase of the Shrine of the Book. The showcase is in the shape of the top of the rod around which Torah scrolls are rolled.

First five columns of the Great Isaiah Scroll, Isaiah 1:1 – 6:7

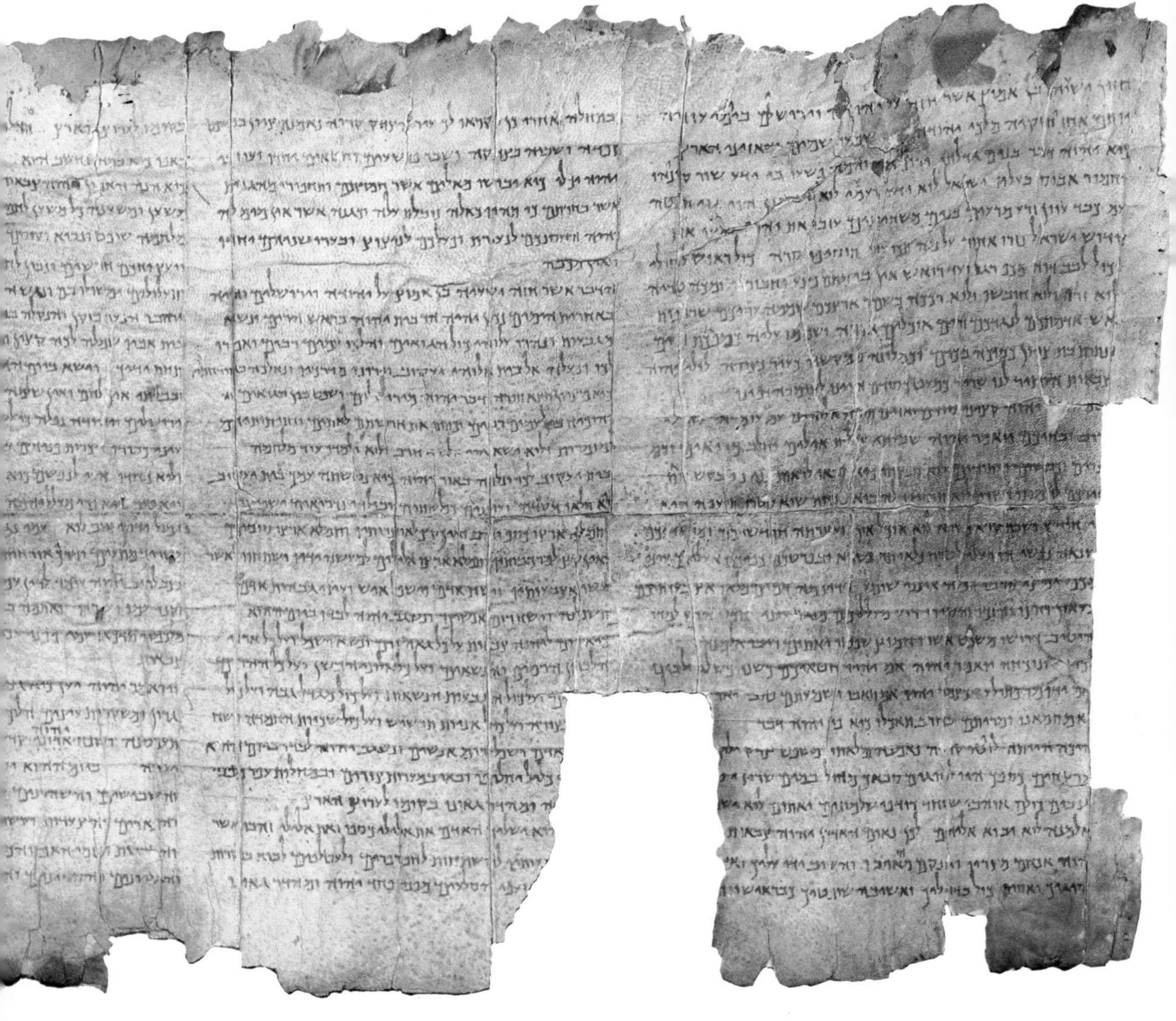

The Biblical Scrolls

The eight Qumran scrolls hold pride of place in Jerusalem's Shrine of the Book; and the two biblical scrolls of Isaiah are undoubtedly the prize of the collection. It is not simply that they are old and unique: this would have given them monetary value but not necessarily importance. Their special significance lies in the fact that their date is known with certainty, and that being a thousand years older than any previously known Hebrew biblical text puts them only about six centuries away from the time the prophet Isaiah uttered his sublime words. Moreover, they were being copied in Qumran long before the codification of the Hebrew text of the Bible.

To appreciate the full import of these facts, one need only recall how the present text came down to us. The original tongue in which the Bible was written was Hebrew. The Hebrew alphabet had no vowel points, and furthermore the biblical texts had no punctuation. There were no commas, no periods to indicate the end of sentences and no capital letters to denote their beginning. (The punctuation and vocalization systems were introduced only in the 8th century C.E.) A good knowledge of grammar was required to read and understand a text accurately. (This is also true of modern Hebrew.) Thus, from quite early times there developed a strict tradition for the faithful transmission of each letter and word of the hallowed writings, together with their pronunciation, from one generation to the next.

However, despite the stringent rules governing the task of copying the biblical documents, performed by skilled scribes who were also accomplished scholars, the factor of human fallibility could not be discounted. It was therefore always thought probable that innocent errors and distortions might have crept into the sacred scrolls as copy followed copy over the centuries. The dream of biblical scholars was to come upon early documents, closer to the first millennium B.C.E. dates of the original Books, to see whether they were different in any substantial way from the Masoretic (traditional) text of the Bible as laid down in the Hebrew canon and as we know it today. This dream had now become a reality, and it explains the excitement that attended the discovery of the Dead Sea documents.

Almost as exciting was a second discovery, made after a thorough examination of the two Isaiah scrolls: there *are* differences between these and the Hebrew text of Isaiah read and studied today in synagogues and Jewish seminaries throughout the world. They also differ somewhat from each other. But the differences are so slight as to make the texts virtually identical. There are minor variations in the spelling, an occasional interchange of words, at times the addition or absence of a phrase. For example, Verse 15 of Chapter 1 in the Masoretic text ends with the phrase: "your hands are full of blood". The scroll acquired by Yadin adds: "and your fingers with crime". Chapter 2, Verse 3, of today's Bible reads: "...let us go up to the mountain of the Lord, to the House of the God of Jacob". The Qumran scroll drops "to the mountain of the Lord". This scroll also omits "therefore forgive them not" in Chapter 2, Verse 9, as well as the whole of the following verse.

Of course, even the slightest change is of importance to scholars anxious to trace the basis of the standard text as we know it. But it is surely remarkable that with all the opportunities for textual variants in successive copies since the prophetic words were first delivered, our current text of Isaiah is much the same as that written in Qumran some 2,100 years ago. Indeed, even the paragraph and chapter divisions in these two Isaiah scrolls, represented by one or more line-spaces, correspond in almost every case to the divisions in the present-day text. So strong was the oral and written tradition of Judaism that the text of the Hebrew Bible — certainly after the canon was established — was handed down from rabbi to student, from scribe to scribe and from father to son with meticulous accuracy in every generation.

But what of the pre-canonical period? The establishment of the Hebrew canon was long held by most scholars to have occurred between 70 C.E. and 132 C.E., namely, during the period from the fall of Jerusalem and the establishment of a new rabbinical centre at Yavne, to the outbreak of the Bar Kochba revolt. It was at Yavne that Rabbi Akiva and his colleagues were said to have determined the definitive list of Books that were to be included in the Hebrew Bible and the accepted standard text of each. Today, however, many scholars believe that the determination of the canon evolved over a longer period. All agree, however, that the content of the Hebrew Bible was fixed after 70 C.E., namely, after the

North-western part of Khirbet Qumran, view to west ▷

Qumran period. Since, therefore, the texts of the biblical Qumran scrolls were all pre-Masoretic, the important question was how they compared with the subsequent canonical text.

We have seen that in the case of the two Isaiah scrolls their texts are followed closely by the Masoretic, showing that the textual tradition of this prophetic work was solid even in pre-Masoretic centuries. Was this also true of the other biblical books?

This was thought to be very likely during the few years when the Isaiah scrolls were the sole discovery amongst Qumran biblical documents. It was possible to give a definite answer, however, only with the later discovery in other Qumran caves of scrolls and fragments belonging to all but one of the biblical books. It was then found that while most, like Isaiah, were closely matched by the Masoretic text, several were not. Some showed that different versions of the same book had co-existed in the Qumran library. The two most notable textual variants were fragments of a "Samaritan-type" Bible, a popular amplified text of the Pentateuch (but without its additional sectarian writings); and the original Hebrew text that had served as the basis of the third-to-second century B.C.E. Greek translation of the Hebrew Bible, the Septuagint. (This, the first translation of the pre-canonical Jewish Scripture, had been initiated by the Greek-speaking Jewish community of Alexandria.)

A number of such variant texts were found among the Qumran manuscripts in the caves discovered in 1952, particularly in Cave 4. For example, there were considerable portions of three scrolls of Jeremiah in this cave. The texts of two of them are much the same as the Masoretic. The third, however, believed to be part of an earlier manuscript, about 200 B.C.E., has a more abbreviated text, lacking several verses that appear in the other two. It follows, indeed, the shorter version of the Book of Jeremiah in the Septuagint, and could well have been a copy of a Hebrew text like that used by the Septuagint translators. Another example is a manuscript of Numbers, where the text seems to be a mixture of the Samaritan and Septuagint types. And in the best preserved portion of a scroll from Cave 4, one of three copies of Samuel, some parts read like the Masoretic text, but rather more follow the Septuagint.

Isaiah 2: 3–4 in the Isaiah Scroll (right) and in the Revised Standard Version (Below)

"Come, let us go up to the mountain of the LORD,
    to the house of the God of Jacob;
that he may teach us his ways
    and that we may walk in his paths."
For out of Zion shall go forth the law,
    and the word of the LORD from Jerusalem.
He shall judge between the nations,
    and shall decide for many peoples;
and they shall beat their swords into ploughshares,
    and their spears into pruning hooks;
nation shall not lift up sword against nation,
    neither shall they learn war any more.

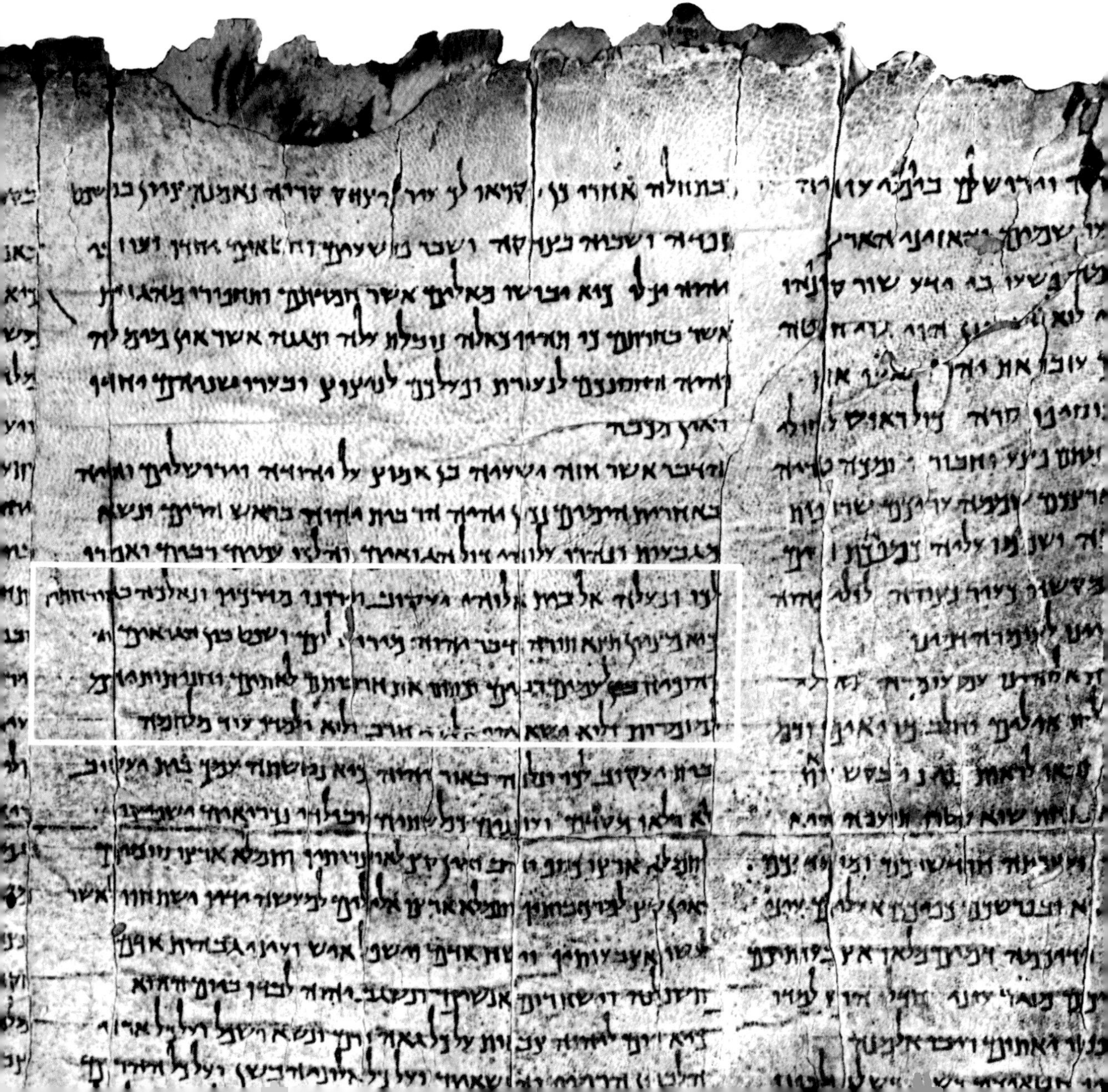

The Biblical Scrolls

Following the establishment of the canon, the Jews discarded texts which varied from the Masoretic, just as they did with works previously considered sacred that nevertheless were excluded from the Hebrew canonical list. These original Hebrew texts soon disappeared. But a number of the works themselves were preserved in translation by certain Christian denominations, such as the books of what was later called the Apocrypha. These, incidentally, had been included in the Septuagint, which had been adopted centuries later as the standard Greek Old Testament of the early Church. Now, with the Qumran discoveries, some of these works had suddenly been brought to light in their language of origin — Hebrew.

The text of the Isaiah scroll acquired in New York from Mar Athanasius Samuel is set out in fifty-four columns, written on seventeen leather sheets sewn together with linen thread. The total length of this scroll is twenty-four feet. Its date is generally accepted to be about 100 B.C.E. The sewing of two tears and the patching of a third attest to its having been much read and studied during its one hundred and seventy years at Qumran before it was hidden. We shall call it Isaiah a. (For readers who wish to go more deeply into the subject, it is well to know that it is referred to in the scroll literature as 1QIsa[a], the 1 standing for Cave 1; Q for Qumran, since manuscript caves were also found in other areas near the Dead Sea; Isa for Isaiah; and the other "a" above the line for the number of the copy.)

The second Isaiah copy, known as 1QIsa[b], was both incomplete and in poor condition when acquired by Sukenik for the Hebrew University. The leather of several sheets had decomposed and the columns were stuck together, so that it was very difficult to unroll. However, the task was accomplished through the care and specialist skills of a Jerusalem expert, J. Bieberkraut, working under Sukenik's supervision, and the writing on the decayed parts became legible in infra-red photographs. Altogether, this scroll contained fragments of thirty-nine chapters, and from these it was possible to discern that in text and spelling it is closer to the Masoretic than is the first Isaiah scroll. It was also copied about 100 years after the first scroll, belonging to the end of the first century B.C.E. or the beginning of the first century C.E.

Prof. Bieberkraut unrolling the Thanksgiving Scroll

The Non-biblical Scrolls

While the Isaiah scrolls are copies of the prophetic text that was included in the Hebrew Bible, the remaining six of the eight scrolls in the Shrine of the Book are non-biblical. One is a paraphrase of certain chapters in the Bible, one is part-biblical and part-sectarian, and four are wholly sectarian — original, hitherto unknown writings by ideologists of the Dead Sea sect, composed during the first century B.C.E. or in the following century. They reveal much that is new about the history of the Qumran period — the dramatic events as well as the conflicting ideas prevalent among the Jews in the final turbulent centuries of the Second Temple and the opening decades of Christianity. A few also provide a detailed record of the codes, concepts and pattern of living of the sect itself.

The titles by which they are known were given by the scholars who worked on them: The Temple Scroll, by Yigael Yadin; The Habakkuk Commentary and The Manual of Discipline, by Millar Burrows; The Thanksgiving Scroll, by E.L. Sukenik; The War of the Sons of Light against the Sons of Darkness, by Sukenik, though the major study was carried out after his death by Yadin; and the Genesis Apocryphon, by Yadin together with Nahman Avigad.

Part of the Thanksgiving Scroll, fragment 2, photographed in ordinary light (left) and infrared light (right)

The Genesis Apocryphon Scroll before unrolling

The Temple Scroll

One of the most important of the sectarian scrolls is the Temple Scroll, acquired by Yadin from a local dealer in 1967. (Incidentally, this was not found with the other seven scrolls in Cave 1, but later, in Cave 11.) It is the longest scroll of all, measuring twenty-eight feet, as against the twenty-four feet of the first Isaiah manuscript. It is also among the more ancient of the Qumran sectarian texts, having been copied in the first century B.C.E. from the original which was composed towards the end of the second century B.C.E., not long after the sect had established itself on the Dead Sea shore.

The Temple Scroll is a Hebrew work which gives the sect's own particular — and harsh — interpretation of the Laws of Moses on several specific subjects, an interpretation different from that followed later by rabbinic Judaism. It echoes the bitter conflict between this breakaway group and the religious authorities in Jerusalem. The style of writing reveals an attempt by the author to copy the language of the Pentateuch, with the Lord quoted in the first person.

The document covers five main topics: the construction and ritual of an idealized Temple; the celebration of additional religious festivals; sacrifices; the laws of purity; and directives to be followed by an ideal Israelite king on, among other themes, the organization and mobilization of the armed forces.

The Temple of Jerusalem, the centre of Jewish religious worship, was still standing when this scroll was written — it was destroyed by the Romans only some two hundred years later. But the Qumran sect did not take part in its services, railing against the priests for their religious laxity, and for failing in their Temple duties to observe to the letter the high standards of purity prescribed in the Torah.

The most significant practical rather than theological difference with the Jerusalem priesthood was their adoption of a different calendar. This brought about a severe rupture, for it meant that a fast-day or a festival being observed by all the other Jews was treated as an ordinary workday by members of the sect. This applied even to Yom Kippur, the most solemn day in the Jewish calendar. The sect's laws governing festivals and fasts, including their own special dates, are laid down in this Temple Scroll.

The Temple Scroll, partly unrolled

The Temple Scroll

Of considerable interest, particularly to the people of Israel today, is the section on the army. One passage in this two-thousand-year-old Hebrew scroll deals with the stage-by-stage recruitment of the nation in ancient Israel when faced with an enemy threat. The scroll prescribes that "if the king learns of any nation and people seeking to take away violently anything that belongs to Israel, he shall send unto the captains of thousands and of hundreds stationed in the cities of Israel, and they shall send to him one tenth of the hosts [reservists] to go with him to war against their enemies...". But if the threat is more serious, and "if a great host comes against the land of Israel, they shall send him one fifth of the men of war". If the "great host" is armed with "chariot and horse", then "one third" of the reservists should be called up and sent to the front, "and the two thirds that are left shall keep ward at their cities and the borders so that no company shall come into their land". And if the situation becomes desperate, and "the battle goes sorely with him [the king], they shall send him one half of the host" to reinforce the combat units, while the other half of the reserve force maintains regional defence.

The leather sheets of this lengthy scroll contain sixty-seven columns of writing. Parts of them, however, were damaged during the years after the discovery of the scroll and before it was acquired by Israel. To ensure the preservation of this and other scrolls, the lighting in the Shrine of the Book is subdued, and temperature and humidity are carefully controlled.

Reconstruction of the inner court of the Temple according to the Temple Scroll
Proposed by Prof. Y. Yadin, drawn by Leen Ritmeyer

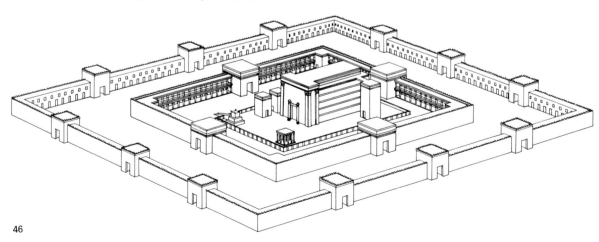

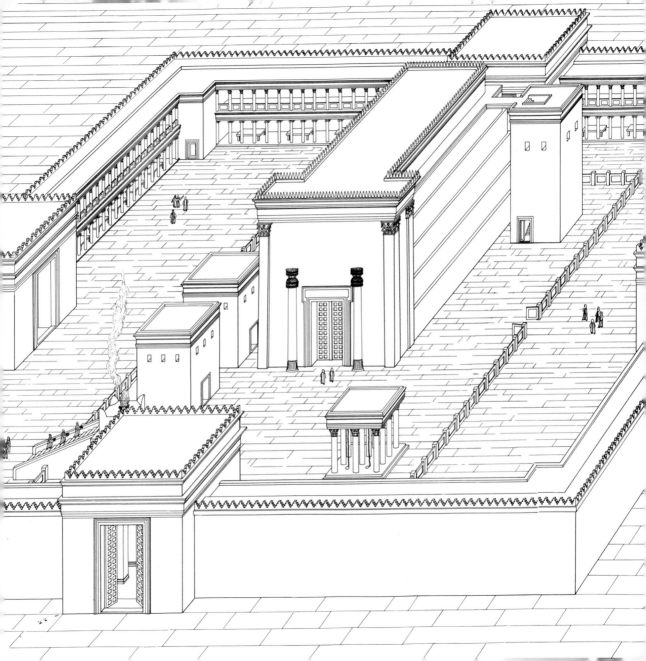

והתם טיבו ארם והבם ארץ קויה ועל ו

פשר הדבר על הכוהן הרשע לשלם לו א

גמו לו אשר גבל על אביונים טא ד לבנון

עצת הדוחד והבודמת הפך פתו והודוד ע

התודה אשר ושופטו אל לכלה

באשר זמם לכלות אביונים יאשר אמר מ

קויה והבם ארץ פשרו הקרוה היא ודי

אשר פעל בו בוו הכוהן מעשו תועבות ויטמא

בקדוש אל והבם ארץ חבה ערי יהודה

חין אביונך בו הועיל נסל טא פני

במ בה יבגרו שקר טא בטוח יער יעד

לעשות אלולים אלמם פשר הדבר על

באלי הגוים אשר יצרם יעובדים ו

להבוח ומה לוא יצולם בוום החפט

ץ אין עד

לה להם הדעת עבד

משקח רשוהי מפחח

לבעג הבבט אל מערוודם

על הכוהן הרשע אשר

ך הצדיק לגלוט בבעס

ו ובקץ מועצ מנוחת

ך הופיע אליהם לבלעם

עם שבת מנוחתם שבעתה

תה עם אתה והדעל

ום ומון עצב וקיקלון

חן אשר גבר קלוט מכבוד

את עוד לת לבו וולך טירנו

פת הצערת וטט חמת

ו ובאעב

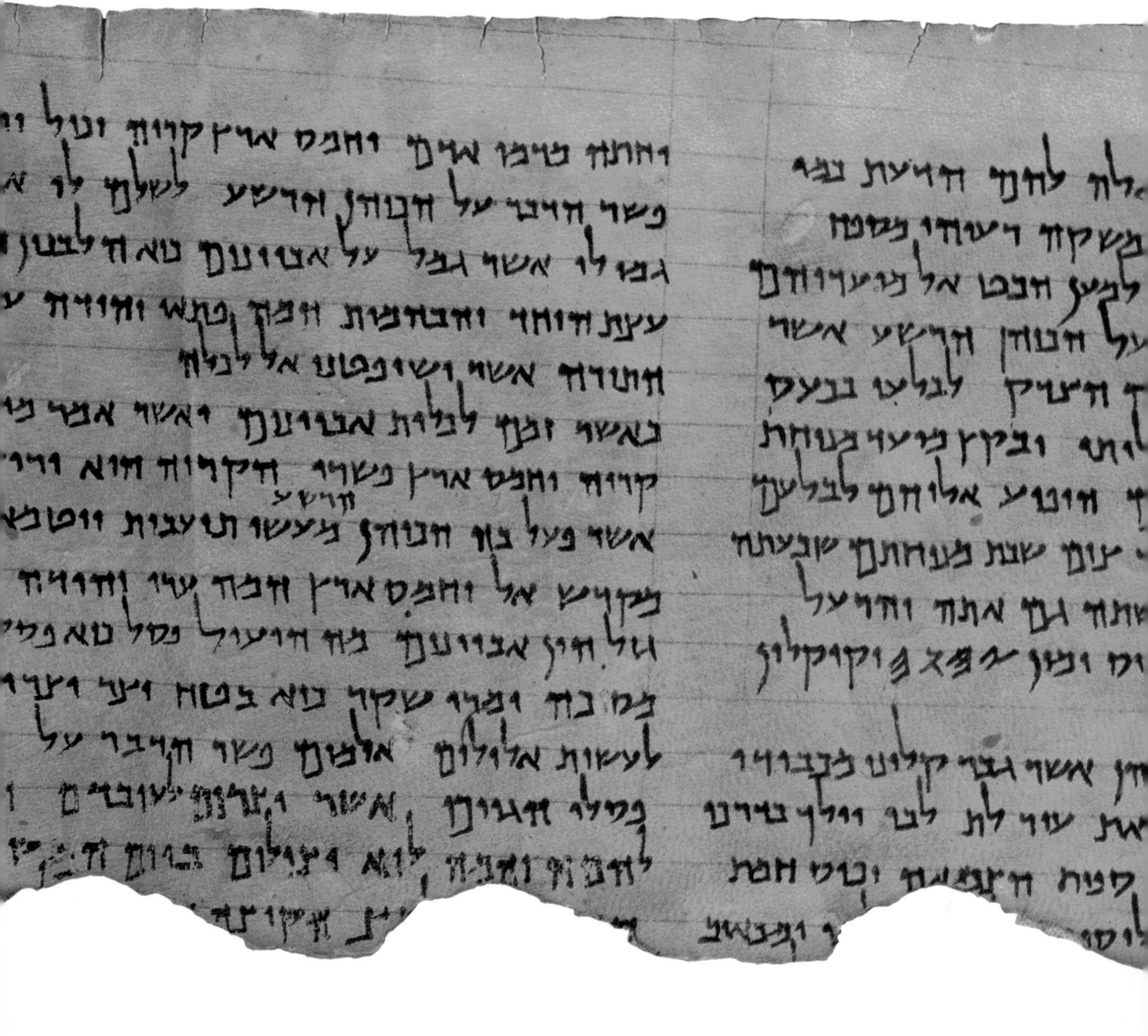

להיות מבעות בעשק ונכסים עלו בחמס ואשר

אשר קצות עמים וכול וחוטאו נפשכה

× את אל יתן אשר המשפט בית הוא פשרו

משפטו בתוך עמים רבים ומשם יעלנו למשפט

חוי ישפטנו ובאש גופרית ירשיענו ובתוכם

הלוא בעולה קריה ויכונן בדמים עיר בונה

הנה מעם ... צבאות ויגעו עמים בדי אש

ולאמים בדי ריק ויעפו

פשרו הדבר על מטיף הכזב אשר התעה רבים

בשקר עדה ולקום בדמים שוו עיר לבנות

בעבור כבודה לוגע רבים בעבודת שוו ולהרותם

בר ... שקר להיות עמלם לריק בעבור יבואו

אל בחירו את ויחרפו גדפו אשר אש למשפטי

אל כבוד את לדעת הארץ תמלא כיא

ונדעו על ...

כשר הדבר

The Habakkuk Commentary

The Habakkuk Commentary is in a category of its own, being part biblical and part sectarian. It is a Hebrew manuscript, four and half feet in length, which quotes the whole of Chapters One and Two of the Book of the prophet Habakkuk, and follows each verse or phrase with a sectarian commentary which the writer calls "its hidden interpretation". In this interpretation, he applies the biblical prophecies to contemporary events. There is thus a dual significance to this scroll. It contains a text from Habakkuk which, like the Isaiah scrolls, is one thousand years closer to the time of the prophet than any previously known text of this biblical Book. And, through its allegorical interpretations, it throws fresh light on the concerns of troubled Judea in the period of the Qumran author, and on the special preoccupations of the sect.

The theme of this scroll and the author's imaginative method of presenting it may best be illustrated by the following example.

The early verses in Chapter One of Habakkuk read: "For lo, I am rousing the Chaldeans, that bitter and hasty nation, who march through the breadth of the earth, to seize habitations not their own. Dread and terrible are they... Their horses are swifter than leopards... They all come for violence; terror of them goes before them... At kings they scoff, and of rulers they make sport" (Habakkuk 1:6–10).

By "the Chaldeans", Habakkuk had in mind the Babylonians — inhabitants of ancient Chaldea — and he uttered his prophecies shortly after they had defeated the Egyptians at the crucial battle of Carchemish in 605 B.C.E. The Babylonians had thereby become the new super-power of the Middle East. The Qumran author was writing six centuries later, when the great power in the region was now the Romans, whom he refers to as "the Kittim". Suiting Habakkuk's words to his own times, he adds this commentary to the above verses: Their "hidden interpretation refers to the Kittim, the fear and terror of whom are on all nations... who trample the land with their horses..."

Having laid the groundwork — substituting "Kittim" for the prophet's "Chaldeans" to describe the power of Rome — the author addresses himself directly to his main purpose: predicting dire punishment for the priestly body in Jerusalem who persecute the Qumran sect. The divine instrument chosen to

Two pottery jars found with the first seven scrolls

The Habakkuk Commentary

inflict that punishment is the Romans, just as the Lord raised the Chaldeans to chastise the evil ones in Habakkuk's day. The author bases himself on Chapter 2 of the prophetic Book. He quotes Verse 2: "Because thou hast spoiled many nations, all the remnant of the peoples shall spoil thee." He then adds: "Its hidden interpretation refers to the last priests of Jerusalem, who gathered wealth and loot from the spoils of the people, but at the end of the days their wealth with their spoil will be given unto the hands of the army of the Kittim."

His principal target is "the Wicked Priest who pursued the Teacher of Righteousness [leader of the Qumran sect] to the house of his exile that he might confuse him with his venomous fury". This is the "hidden interpretation" of Verses 5–7 of Habakkuk Chapter 2, where the prophet speaks of a greedy and "arrogant man" whose desire "is as death, and cannot be satisfied... Woe to him that increaseth that which is not his!... Will not your debtors suddenly arise... who will make you tremble? Then you will be booty for them".

When this Habakkuk Commentary scroll was discovered and studied, it was unique. No other document of this nature was known to scholars. Later excavations in the area of Qumran, however, yielded parts of similarly styled "commentaries" on other biblical Books, the most important of which were two fragments, one on the Psalms and the other on the prophet Nahum. There is enough text on these few pieces of leather to show that both use the same device as that in the Habakkuk Commentary — giving an allegorical meaning to a biblical document. The composers, however, may have genuinely believed they were interpreting biblical prophecy in terms of the history of their sect, which they saw as the history of the true Israel.

Furniture (partially reconstructed) from the Qumran scriptorium, probably benches used by the scribes

Abecedarium – a scribal exercise on a potsherd

The Thanksgiving Scroll

The Qumran-Jerusalem conflict is also reflected in another sectarian scroll, one of the three acquired by Sukenik. It consists of a group of personal hymns, the author's songs of praise to the Lord. Written in Hebrew and somewhat similar in style, though not in content, to the biblical Psalms, most of them begin with "I thank thee, O Lord", and Sukenik therefore entitled the collection The Thanksgiving Scroll (IQM).

This leather document was difficult to unroll, for it appeared to have been much used and already in poor condition by the time it was hastily concealed, and the leather sheets had begun to decay, producing a dark excretion. They were quite stiff and stuck together when discovered, and it took endless work by J. Bieberkraut before the full length of the scroll was unrolled. Eighteen columns have been preserved, though the top and some of the lower margins are eroded, and there are some seventy additional fragments (as well as other copies from Cave 4). Most of the columns, as in the other scrolls, are legible to the naked eye, but the text of others could be read only with the help of infra-red photography. The original length of the scroll is estimated to have been ten feet.

It is evident from the Hebrew script that this was one of the later Qumran documents, having been copied in the first century C.E. And from the autobiographical references in some of the hymns, Sukenik concluded that the author was the "Teacher of Righteousness" himself. He thanks the Lord for sheltering him from "the violent who seek my soul / because I adhere to Thy Covenant", and for strengthening him in his struggle against the sinful "congregation of Belial".

It is he, the author, who feels himself the recipient of divine inspiration, while the priests in Jerusalem are "interpreters of lies and prophets of guile", who "formed plots against me... Wanting me to barter Thy law which Thou has engraved on my heart / For the flatteries which they address to Thy people".

Part of the Thanksgiving Scroll before opening

The Manual of Discipline

The sectarian scrolls discussed so far appear to have been written by a Dead Sea group concerned with their own extremist interpretation of the sacred books which were eventually included in the Hebrew Bible, and this put them at odds with the priests and community in Jerusalem. But their beliefs, and particularly the code of rules by which they lived, are known to us chiefly through another sectarian scroll, also written in Hebrew, discovered with the others. This is the Manual of Discipline (IQS) which sets forth the rules of membership of this pious sect, presents their religious principles, and describes their pattern of living. Its eleven columns written on five sheets of parchment give it a length of just over six feet. Marginal amendments and later editorial alterations suggest that it was in use over a long period, having been written, according to the style of the script, at the beginning of the first century B.C.E., though the original work of which this was a copy is believed to have been composed in the latter half of the previous century. (Parts of other copies of the Manual were also found in Cave 4 and Cave 5.)

Geza Vermes, in his admirable book *The Dead Sea Scrolls: Qumran in Perspective,* says the Manual "appears to have served as a handbook of instruction for the Master or Guardian of the community".

The scroll opens with the initiation rites of new members. The ceremony requires an oath to uphold the principles of the Qumran faith, and to respect the divine laws given "through Moses and through all his servants, the prophets"; to live with truth and righteousness and to spurn evil; to adhere to the special calendar of the sect; not to be deterred by any action that might be taken by "the dominion of Belial"; and to contribute "all their knowledge and strength and wealth" to the community.

Candidates who are accepted become "Sons of Light", pledged "to hate all Sons of Darkness", and the Manual goes on to explain that the Lord in His wisdom made for man "two spirits by which to walk" until the end of days. "They are the spirits of Truth and Perversion." Truth dwells "in the abode of Light", and perversion in the abode of Darkness. But the Lord "has fixed a period" for perversion, and at the appointed time "He will destroy it for ever". The sect believed that this time was near.

A cistern, probably used as a ritual bath

The Manual of Discipline

The code governing them shows that theirs was a disciplined communal existence. "Together they shall eat and together they shall pray; together they shall counsel." At meetings, there were to be no interruptions: "A man shall not speak in the midst of his neighbour's words". There was also to be no questioning of authority: "A man shall not speak a word which is not to the liking of the superiors".

Another section of the Manual is devoted to judgement and punishment of errant members. Anyone found to have lied about his wealth was to be penalized by one year's isolation, and deprived of a quarter of his rations. There was a similar punishment for insulting one of the community's priests. Three months was the penalty for uttering an obscenity. Interrupting a speaker brought ten days, and spitting "in the middle of the public session will be punished thirty days". There is an interesting amendment to the punishment for "one who bears a grudge against a fellow without justification". The original script called for a six-months sentence. The insertion above the words "six months" was "a year", presumably added later by a harsh Guardian.

The Manual makes clear that these were the rules by which members were to conduct themselves during the reign of the "Dominion of Belial" — the religious establishment in Jerusalem. But that reign would soon end, and the scroll formulates the communal regulations that are to prevail "at the end of days", including preparations for the final battle against the forces of evil.

Qumran – an artist's reconstruction of the community's center

1 Main entrance
2 Defense tower
3 Scriptorium
4 Refectory
5 Potter's workshop
6 Entrance to aqueduct
7 Reservoirs
8 Animal pen
9 Entrance from fields

Reconstruction by Leen Ritmeyer

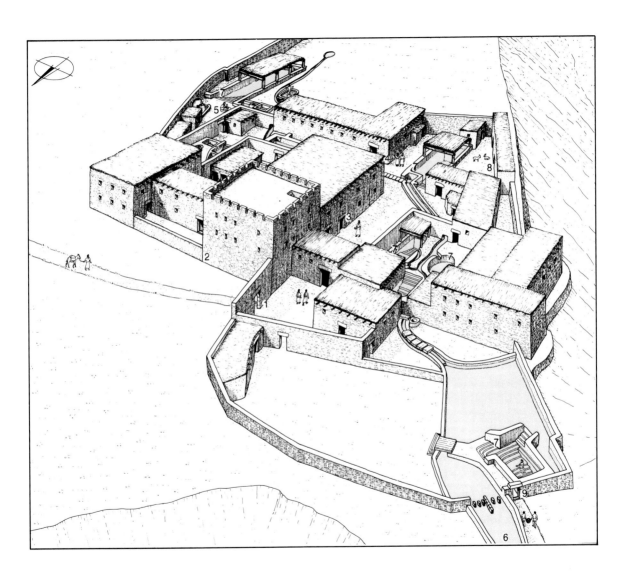

The War Scroll

Preparations for the final battle mentioned in The Manual of Discipline, including planning, organization and mobilization, are set out in detail in another sectarian scroll known as The War of the Sons of Light against the Sons of Darkness. Though much of the text reads like a military handbook, with sections on strategy, unit formations and weaponry, it is primarily a religious work, an eschatological treatise concerned with the forces of good and evil that would clash on the battlefield in a great and final war "at the end of days". (Here, as scholars were quick to note, was an echo of the idea of the eschatological war in chapters 37 and 38 of Ezekiel.) The war, according to the scroll, would last forty years, with victory — and salvation — going to the righteous through divine intervention. The righteous are the Sons of Light, the people who accept the rules and beliefs of the Qumran sect. But the Sons of Darkness who are to be vanquished are now not only the priestly body and community in Jerusalem but also the neighbouring countries, the traditional enemies of Israel since biblical times, as well as the "Kittim", the all-powerful Romans.

This nine-foot scroll, one of the three purchased by Sukenik, contains nineteen columns of beautiful Hebrew script written on five leather sheets, their lower margins left ragged through erosion. Each column, or page, bore an average of twenty lines, and still visible were the indentations of the stylus used by the scribe to rule the pages, horizontal lines for the text, and vertical lines to separate the columns. The end of a paragraph was denoted by the space of a line. The last page of the manuscript is missing. The work was composed at the end of the first century B.C.E. or beginning of the following century. (The remains of four additional manuscripts of this book were discovered later in other Qumran caves.)

The forty-year war envisaged by the writer, to be fought in stages, would be against the gentile neighbouring enemy nations of "Edom and Moab and the Sons of Ammon and the army of the dwellers of Philistia", as well as the "Kittim". These are the external foes. But in league with them will be "the offenders against the Covenant", meaning the enemies of the Sons of Light from within the Jewish community. All fall under the heading of the Sons of Darkness. Fighting

The War Scroll, column III, with scribal correction visible above line 1

סרך חצוצרות מקראיה בפרואף בהכונה שערי המלחמה לצאת אנשי הבנף וחצוצרות תרועת חללים וחלים וחצוצרות

המארב וחצוצרות הרדף בהנגף אויב וחצוצרות המאסף בשוב המלחמה על חצוצרות מקרא העדה יכתובו קרואי אל

ועל חצוצרות מקרא חני שרים יכתובו נשיאי אל ועל חצוצרות המסרות יכתובו סרף אל ועל חצוצרות אנשי

השם ראשי אבות . . . רוח ...יחד בהאספם לבית מועד יכתובו תעודות אל לעצת קודש ועל חצוצרות המועדת

יכתובו שלום אל בבחני קרושוו ועל חצוצרות מסעיהם יכתובו גבורות אל לחפנץ אויב ולהניס כל משנאי

צרק ומשוב חסדים במשנאי אל ועל חצוצרות סדרי המלחמה יכתובו וצאו סררי וצאא אל לעקמת אפ בכל בני חושך

ועל חצוצרות מקרא אנשי חכנום כהפתח שערי המלחמה לצאת למערכת האויב יכתובו זכרון בעם בם בקיער

אל ועל חצוצרות החללים יכתובו יד גבורת אל במלחמה להפיל כל חללי מעל ועל חצוצרות המארב יכתובו

רזי אל לשחתת רשעה ועל חצוצרות המרדף יכתובו נגף אל כל בני חושך לוא ישוב אפו עד כלותם

ובשובם מן המלחמה לבוא המערכת יכתובו על חצוצרות המשוב אסף אל ועל חצוצרות דרף המשוב

מבלחמת האויב לבוא אל העיר ירושלם יכתובו גילות אל במשוב שלום

סרך אותותבל העדה למסורותם על האות הגדולה אשר בראש כל עם יכתובו עם אל ואת שם ישראל

ואהרון ושמות שנים עשר שבטי ...לתולדותם ראשי העדות אשר לשלושיו וחמשום

...בש ...וש וכתובו נשם אל ואת שני נשיאי

...רבבא את שמות שרי אלפיו

The War Scroll

in the army of the Sons of Light are the tribes of Levi, Judah and Benjamin, and "the exiles of the wilderness" — the community in Qumran — and other members of the sect, or their supporters, in the Diaspora.

In presenting the military pattern of the projected war, the author of the scroll had clearly drawn on both the military directives for the battles in the Bible and on the tactics and weapons employed in his own time. Indeed, he appears to have been very familiar with the contemporary military structure. The scroll offers detailed descriptions, for example, of army units — including the appropriate ages of the men to be assigned to light and heavy infantry and cavalry. We are even told the measurements of the weapons they are to use — slings, lances, javelins, spears, swords and shields. One piquant detail is the kind of horses required for the cavalry. They are to be "male horses, fleet of foot, tender of mouth, long of wind... trained for battle and accustomed to noises and to all sights and spectacles".

Both the heavenly and earthly worlds are to be engaged in the war, and the account in the scroll tells of angels and demons playing active roles in the course of the campaign. Nevertheless, there is a practical realism in the descriptions of the combat units — and in the recognition that the Sons of Darkness will put up strong resistance, with the Sons of Light suffering defeats in battle before their ultimate victory in the war. There are accordingly prayers for all occasions, and this beautiful liturgy takes up much of the scroll. There are prayers for the eve of battle, prayers of encouragement to raise morale after a setback, curses for the enemy when the going is tough, praise for the Lord when the combat goes well. There is finally a prayer for when the war is won and the era of Perversion is over. The era of Truth is to be ushered in, "And the Kingdom shall be the Lord's / Over Israel shall be his eternal Dominion".

White dome and black wall of the Shrine of the Book

The Manual of Discipline, column X

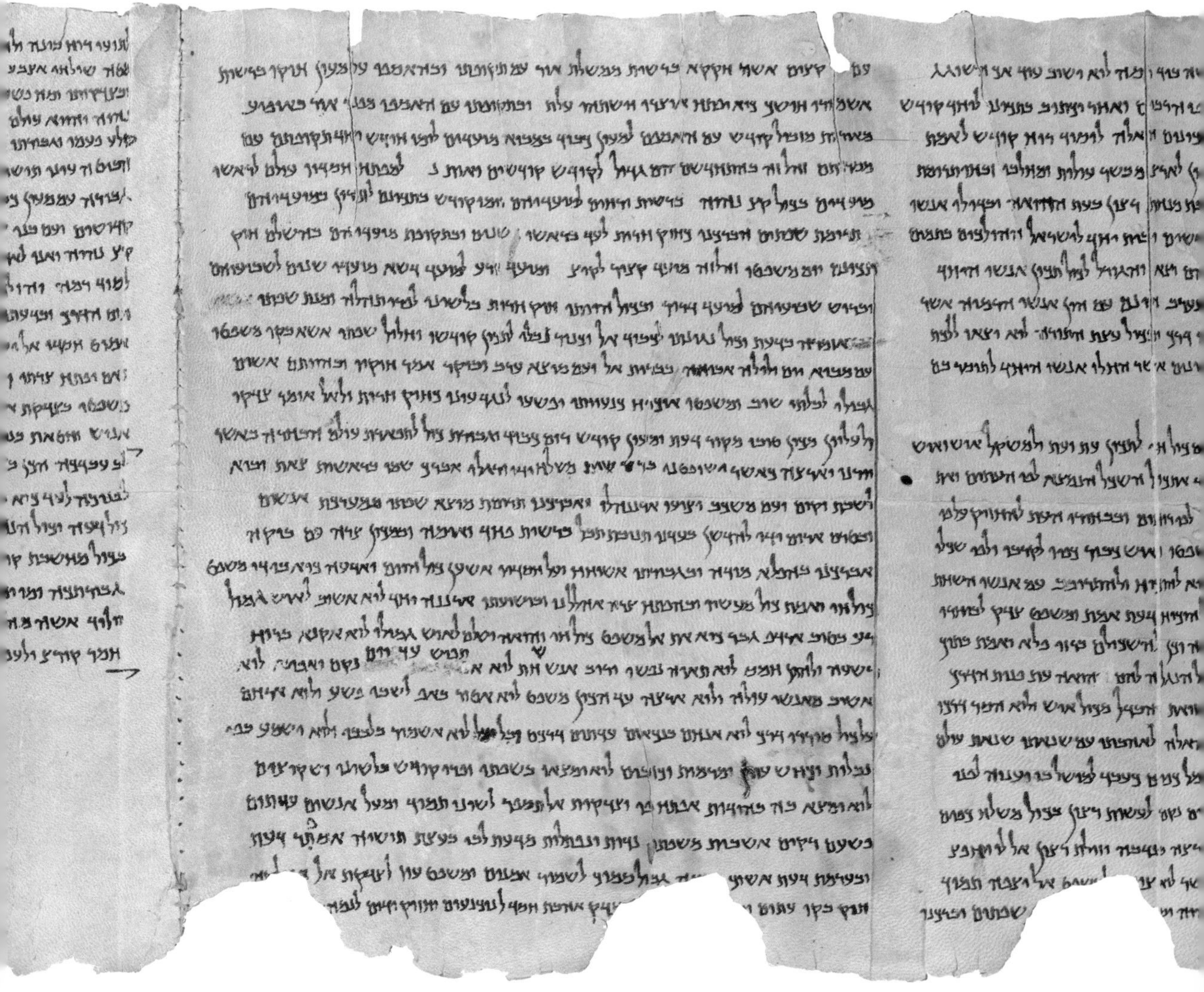

1:1

The open tefillin capsule, with folded slips of scriptural passages

The Genesis Apocryphon

This scroll, unlike the other scrolls, is written not in Hebrew but in Aramaic, the everyday language widely used by Jews in Middle Eastern countries at the time. It is a paraphrase of several chapters of the Book of Genesis, expanded to include colourful details of sparse facts in the original text, as well as additional stories and even new characters.

It is a fascinating literary work which gives the clear impression of having been written by a talented novelist who was also an imaginative scholar, steeped in biblical literature, and seeking to re-create the life and times of the biblical world. The scroll itself was copied in the beginning of the first century B.C.E., but was probably composed in the latter half of the previous century, or even earlier.

It was a difficult document to unroll, having been found in a very fragile state, and Bieberkraut again came to the rescue, attended by Yigael Yadin and Nahman Avigad, the scholars who subsequently deciphered and translated the ancient Aramaic script. It was one of the four scrolls taken to America by the Syrian bishop, but because of its condition had not been unrolled there and so could not be published in facsimile, as were the other three. However, one of its opening sheets had become detached and was examined by American scholar John C. Trever. He discerned that the writing was Aramaic, and deciphered the biblical name of Lamech, the father of Noah. He therefore thought it might well be the Book of Lamech, which received a single mention in an old Greek list of apocryphal books. It was accordingly known as The Lamech Scroll until it reached Jerusalem several years later, was unrolled and examined. It was found to be an apocryphal version of Genesis, supplemented by narratives not unlike those in works which, though excluded from the Bible, continued to be preserved in the Apocrypha.

Lamech appears in the early columns of the scroll which correspond to Chapter 5 of Genesis. But added to the Genesis account is the legend of the miraculous birth of Noah, similar to the one presented in the apocryphal book of Enoch. In this story the beauty of the baby Noah, born to Lamech and his wife Bat-Enosh, leads Lamech to suspect that the child had been sired not by him but by an angel. However, the scroll presents this legend in an unusual way. It has Lamech,

Exhibition corridor of the Shrine of the Book

66

The Genesis Apocryphon

speaking in the first person, acknowledging his fears that "the conception had been from... the holy ones or the fallen angels. And my heart was changed because of this child". Confronting his wife, who "perceived that my countenance had changed", he goes on to record her reassurance "that thine is the seed and from thee is the conception and from thee was the fruit formed" of the child Noah. "And it is no stranger's, nor is it of any of the Watchers or of the Sons of Heaven."

The most interesting part of the scroll is an embroidered version of the chronicles in Chapters 12 to 15 of Genesis, dealing with the early story of Abraham, his arrival and sojourn in Canaan, and his journey to Egypt with his wife Sarah. Genesis related that when Abraham "was come into Egypt, the Egyptians beheld the woman that she was very fair", whereupon Sarah was promptly "taken into Pharaoh's house". She was released and returned to Abraham only after the Lord had smitten the royal household with plagues.

The Genesis Apocryphon picks out the two words in the biblical book describing Sarah as "very fair", and adds this detailed passage on her beauty: "[How] beautiful the look of her face... [how] fine is the hair of her head, how fair indeed are her eyes and how pleasing her nose and all the radiance of her face... How beautiful her breast and how lovely all her whiteness. Her arms goodly to look upon, and her hands how perfect... how fine and long all the fingers of her hands. Her legs how beautiful and how without blemish her thighs... And above all women is she lovely..."

The narrative is presented as Abraham speaking in the first person, but the above description of Sarah's beauty is part of the report given to Pharaoh by his chief prince, whom the scroll calls Horkanosh. The end of the story contains a possible clue to the reason for its inclusion in this scroll. It may be that the author was troubled by Abraham's deception, in the Genesis account, in telling Pharaoh that Sarah was not his wife but his sister. The author of the scroll therefore explains that on his way to Egypt, Abraham has a dream in which he fears he will be murdered when he reaches that country. Sarah alone can save him, and the dream tells him how. The dream is the Lord's way of counselling Abraham, and so it was not a deception by Abraham but a directive from the Lord.

The Tefillin of Qumran

Also on display in the central chamber together with the eight Dead Sea scrolls are a leather capsule and four leather fragments covered by portions of the Bible written in minute but clear Hebrew script, dating back to the beginning of the 1st century C.E. This intriguing find in a Qumran cave was the head-capsule of Tefillin (Phylacteries) and its scriptual texts.

The discovery was unique, for though the remains of empty capsules had been found at Qumran, as well as non-encapsulated stray fragments, here, for the first time, was a head-capsule with three of the four parchment slips bearing biblical texts in their original compartments, exactly as they were when they had been inserted and sealed two thousand years ago.

The remarkable features of these inscribed slips that immediately strike the eye is the smallness of the writing, so tiny indeed that it can be read easily only through a magnifying glass. The scribe had to write such minute characters so that each slip would contain all its required biblical verses; and these slips had to be small because the capsules in turn had to be small, for in those days the Tefillin were worn by many throughout the day, and not, as now, during the morning prayers alone.

The talmudic sages had devoted much study to the technical details concerning the Tefillin, and the rabbinical literature contains regulations ranging from the scriptural verses to be used, the parchment on which they were to be written and the order in which they were to be placed inside the capsules, down to the materials with which the capsules themselves were to be fashioned, and the thread with which the inscribed slips were to be tied when placed within their compartments. Now that this preserved head-capsule and writings had come to light, it was possible to compare them with the rabbinic prescriptions — and clear up obscurities in some of the puzzling passages of the Talmud.

After careful examination, including laboratory tests, it was found that the physical features accorded with the talmudic regulations. The capsule was made of calf-leather. It had four moulded recesses — compartments for the parchment slips — and a tubular space for the straps running along the base of the compartments. The stitching to seal each compartment and the capsule itself was with thread made of animal tendons. The inscribed slips were kid-skin

Tefillin slip no. 3 after opening, with verses from Deuteronomy 5: 1–21 and Exodus 13: 11–16
Below: original size

of a rare thinness — 0.04 millimeters — which were folded in a special way and tied with goat-hair.

The writings, on the other hand, were definitely at variance with rabbinic tradition. While each slip contained one of the four basic biblical paragraphs prescribed by that tradition, all also had additional verses from the same two Books, Exodus and Deuteronomy. The basic paragraphs were : in slip One, Exodus 13:1–10; slip Two, Deuteronomy 6:4–9; slip Three, Exodus 13:11–16; and slip Four is presumed to have included Deuteronomy 11:13–21. (Slip Four did not belong to the original capsule. It was a stray Tefillin fragment that was probably inserted into this capsule by the Bedouin who found it or the antiquities dealer from whom it was acquired, when the fourth compartment was found to be empty.) All four paragraphs contain references similar to the "sign upon your hand" and "frontlets between your eyes" that appear in the "Hear, O Israel" passage in Deuteronomy. The additional biblical verses were: in slip One, Exodus 12:43–51 and Deuteronomy 10:12–19; slip Two, Deuteronomy 5:22–33 and 6:1–3; and slip Three, Deuteronomy 5:1–21. Slip Four was too fragmented and the writing too ill-preserved for the text to be identified with certainty.

It appears that during the 1st century C.E. there were varied customs relating to the selection of the Tefillin texts; but at the beginning of the 2nd century the rabbinic decision fixed these texts as consisting of the four basic passages, without any addition of such verses as those in these Tefillin.

As to the order in which the texts were to be placed inside the capsule, this was a subject of controversy among the rabbis, and, indeed, two traditions remained even after the textual uniformity decision — and they persist to this day. They are associated with the notable controversy between the outstanding 11th century talmudic and biblical commentator, Rashi, and his distinguished grandson, Rabbenu Tam. While the tradition expressed by Rashi is followed by most communities today, there are others who wear "the Tefillin of Rabbenu Tam". The order of the Tefillin in the Shrine of the Book is closer to that of Rashi's, the only difference being the transposition of the texts on the inner slips Two and Three.

Of special interest is the additional passage in slip Three, Deuteronomy 5:1–21, which contains the Ten Commandments; and these Commandments also

The closed tefillin capsule, original size

appear on some of the other Tefillin fragments found at Qumran. Apparently the Decalogue had been part of the regular text of all Tefillin up to the final years of the Second Temple period, but were omitted from the standard rabbinic text established in the 2nd century C.E. The reason for its deletion is suggested in references in the rabbinic literature. These show that while the Decalogue had been recited in the Temple and included in the Tefillin text, the practice was discontinued because of the "hatred of the heretics" — assumed to refer to the early Christian sect — who claimed that it was "these [Ten Commandments] *alone* that were given to Moses in Sinai"!

The acquisition for the Shrine of the Book and the scientific study of the Qumran Tefillin were by Yigael Yadin.

Opening the tefillin

Additional Archaeological Finds

The principal Dead Sea Scrolls had been found by chance by Bedouin goatherds, and the excitement of the scholars lay in deciphering and studying them. But far more satisfying for these scholars was the search for similar ancient documents at their own archaeological excavations. Indeed, apart from the eight scrolls already reviewed, all the other documentary treasures on display in the Shrine of the Book were found by Israeli archaeologists at digs in the Dead Sea area. Each find was the climax to an exhausting — and often daring — physical effort.

Additional Archaeological Finds

Cave of Letters, Nahal Hever

The Caves of Bar Kochba

The first major exploration in Israel with the specific aim of finding further ancient writings was undertaken in 1960 and again in 1961 in what are now known as the caves of Bar Kochba. They are located in the slopes of the wadis running off the Dead Sea between the biblical Judean site of Ein-Gedi and the rock of Masada, lying to the south of Qumran.

Bar Kochba was the Jewish leader who had successfully raised the banner of revolt against the Romans in 132 C.E., sixty-two years after they had destroyed Jerusalem. For the next three years, the Jews again enjoyed independence in their land, with Jerusalem their capital and religious centre. But then the emperor Hadrian sent in his powerfully armed Roman legions, and they proceeded to crush the Jewish outposts one by one. In the closing phases of the bitter campaign, Bar Kochba's resistance fighters sought refuge with their families in the Judean caves.

The first documents relating to Bar Kochba were discovered by Father Roland de Vaux in the late 1950's in Wadi Muraba'at in the north Judean Desert. The assumption that prompted the Israeli exploration was that when Bar Kochba's men realized the end was near, they would probably have hidden their treasured documents beneath the floors or in the walls of the caves. If so, the prospect of recovering them seemed hopeful, since the Qumran scrolls had been found in caves only a short distance away, albeit just within the territory occupied by Jordan. Perhaps a well-directed search of the caves on the Israeli side of the border might yield similar success.

Two modest reconnaissance surveys were accordingly undertaken by archaeologist Yohanan Aharoni in the early and mid-1950s. He found that even those caves that he and his party could reach only with ropes and ladders showed signs of search by Bedouin. World interest in the scrolls, and the huge sums they could fetch, had sent them scurrying among the Dead Sea cliffs on treasure hunts. But in one of the caves where the Bedouin had preceded him — leaving crumpled cigarette packs and other evidence that they had been there — Aharoni came upon gruesome remains from the Bar Kochba period. These were the skeletons of men, women and children, all that was left of the second century fighters and their kin. If they had hidden any sacred works before their death, these had evidently been removed by the Bedouin. Aharoni therefore reported that it might be rewarding to investigate caves which were now inaccessible to the ordinary climber. This, however, would require a large-scale expedition, with appropriate manpower and equipment to reach, enter and excavate caves which had eluded the Bedouin.

The expedition was mounted in 1960–61 by the Hebrew University, the Israel Exploration Society and the Government Department of Antiquities, with the help of technical personnel and equipment from the Israel Defence Forces. The rugged region was divided into four sectors and each was assigned to a separate team headed by an experienced archaeologist. The team leaders were Yohanan Aharoni, Nahman Avigad, Pesach Bar-Adon and Yigael Yadin. Preliminary reconnaissance to select the most promising caves was carried out by army helicopter. Each archaeologist, sitting with the pilot and an air force photographer, was flown through the canyons in his particular sector so that he could survey the cave-openings and crevices in the craggy walls at eye level. All were on the lookout for traces of old trails and narrow goat paths, eroded over the centuries to perilous ledges. Now impassable, in antiquity they might have led to hiding places. The most tempting caves, several as much as three hundred feet below the lip of the summit and one thousand feet above the floor of the gorge, were marked down for investigation.

In the opening days, trial descents to the mouths of the caves were made by paratroop volunteers dangling at the end of ropes and making spot searches. When the indications were hopeful, naval personnel prepared rope ladders picketed to stakes in the plateau above; army engineers widened the approach tracks where possible, and put up guard rails along the narrow ledges, so that archaeologists could reach the caves with less hazard and start excavating inside. There, however, they faced danger from rock-falls, collapsing roofs, and a foetid atmosphere which made work possible only for brief periods at a time. All four teams were successful in finding remains of considerable historical interest. Three discovered writings and dated coins. Aharoni, examining several caves, one more difficult to reach than another, unearthed fragments of

Bronze vessels from the Cave of
Letters, taken booty from Roman
legionnaires

A letter from Bar Kochba to
Joshua, son of Galgola, found in
Wadi Murabba at

The Caves of Bar Kochba

parchment and papyri from a small pit, together with coins and artefacts, and, from under a vulture's nest, more pieces of papyri. The written material included portions of prayers from Tefillin in minute Hebrew script; parchments bearing parts of the Hebrew text of Chapter 13 of Exodus; part of a leather scroll with Hebrew letters;and Hebrew and Greek papyri. Bar-Adon, whose greatest find was a fourth millennium B.C.E. cache of Chalcolithic copper and ivory objects, also found two fragments of papyri, one with Hebrew and the other with Greek writing, both from the Bar Kochba period.

The most fortunate documentary discovery, however, fell to Yadin, and the cave of the find has since become known as the Cave of Letters. The exploration started with a happy omen when one of his team found a coin just outside the entrance which bore a palm tree on one side with the inscription "Shimon", Bar Kochba's first name. The obverse side showed a cluster of grapes and the Hebrew words "Le'Herut Yerushalayim", "For the Freedom of Jerusalem". Then came the find of manuscripts.

One was a parchment fragment in Hebrew of parts of Chapters 15 and 16 of the Book of Psalms. The rest were fifteen battle dispatches in Greek and Aramaic from Bar Kochba at his field headquarters to two of his officers, Yehonatan and Masabala, who appear to have been the military commander and the civil administrator at Ein-Gedi. Excavated from a cavity in a corner of one of the chambers adjacent to the large cave, the documents were wrapped in a kerchief that had been placed in a leather water-skin. All except one were written on papyrus. The exception was a letter written on wood, which had been "folded" into four slats, and inscribed with two columns of Aramaic. It opened with the words: "Shimon bar Kosiba, Prince over Israel, to Yehonatan and Masabala, Shalom". (Bar Kosiba or Kosba is how Shimon Bar Kochba is referred to in rabbinic literature.)

These battlefield messages to Bar Kochba's rear base at Ein-Gedi, written in 134 or 135 C.E., deal largely with mobilization instructions and with supplies. The latter reveal that even amidst the harsh afflictions of a desperate war, Bar Kochba sought scrupulously to fulfil the injunctions of the Torah. One letter, for example, demands the prompt dispatch of "palm branches and citrons... and

Ascent to the Cave of Letters

Bar Kochba bronze coin. The palm tree was a symbol of Judea

myrtles and willows" so that he and his men could celebrate the Festival of Succot with the required "four species" of plant (in accordance with the rabbinic interpretation of Leviticus 23: 39–43). Bar Kochba was even careful enough to add: "Ensure that they are tithed".

Returning the following year for a more thorough excavation of the cave and its ancillary chambers, Yadin discovered many manuscripts in Hebrew, Aramaic, Nabatean and Greek which contribute greatly to the study of the Talmud, philology and the general history of the times. Many of them contain specific dates, which make it possible to fix with certainty the period of an archaeological stratum. One Hebrew papyrus document, for example, is a deed leasing state land, effected through Bar Kochba's administrator in Ein-Gedi, which bears the day, month and year. It begins: "On the 28th day of Marheshvan [the Jewish month roughly corresponding to November], year 3 [corresponding to 135 C.E.] of Shimon ben Kosiba, Prince of Israel..." The information in this deed and others, so valuable to scholars, includes detailed specifications of the leased plots, their boundaries, the crops raised, the water rights and the terms of payment. It is evident that behind the battle zone, Bar Kochba's civil administration sought to preserve the norms of daily living, while keeping supplies flowing to the troops in the field.

A batch of thirty-five papyrus documents (contained in a leather pouch) in Aramaic, Nabatean and Greek, offer facets of civilian life at the end of the first and the beginning of the second century C.E., before the Bar Kochba uprising. They proved to be the family archive belonging to a wealthy woman named Babata. One letter reveals that she was a distant relative of Yehonatan, one of Bar Kochba's two representatives in Ein-Gedi. Presumably, when the end was near, the families fled to the caves, and Babata took her important documents with her. Among the manuscripts are legal papers relating to lawsuits, mortgages, land leases, loans and title deeds. Six of the papyri are in Nabatean, and are of special importance since there had been no previous discovery of Nabatean writing other than inscriptions on rocks and tombs. They were in this language because they deal mostly with property bought by Babata's father in neighbouring Nabatean territory, and all six belong to the end of the first century

Household objects, mirror, jewelry box and keys from the Cave of Letters

Parcel of palm fibres (left) in which
the glass plate (right) was found

The Caves of Bar Kochba

C.E. We know this because they are dated according to the year in the third decade of the thirty-six-year reign of King Rabael II (70–106 C.E.), last of the Nabatean rulers. The kingdom was crushed by the Romans in 106 C.E. and became a province of Rome. The Babata documents thereafter are in Greek and Aramaic. Among the Aramaic is Babata's marriage contract (*ketuba* in Hebrew), declaring that the marriage was to be performed according to "the law of Moses and the Jews". This formula was changed a few years later, during Bar Kochba's rule, to "of Moses and Israel", and this phrase is used in the *ketuba* of a Jewish marriage to this day.

One of the Greek papyri dated eight years before the Bar Kochba revolt is a deed acknowledging a loan to Babata's husband by the commander of the Roman garrison at Ein-Gedi. Yadin suggests that these Roman troops were subdued in the opening stages of the Jewish revolt, and Roman vessels of bronze which he found in the Cave of Letters (and which are also on display in the Shrine of the Book) had probably belonged to this garrison.

Of particular interest are some of the legal papers which use three systems of dating. One records the year of the reign of the Roman emperor; the second notes the names of the consuls of Rome for that year; and the third gives the year since Nabatea was re-named the Arabian Province after the loss of its independence in 106, so that "the fifteenth year of Arabia Provincia" would correspond to 121 C.E. The documents thus offer a complete synchronization of all three systems. Incidentally, several Roman consuls are mentioned whose names had been missing from the Roman lists. Babata's archive filled the gaps. Babata, her family, companions, and the resistance fighters perished shortly after they had hidden their papers when Hadrian's army crushed the revolt. But, as Yadin wrote in his book on the exploration of the Bar Kochba caves, "Archaeologists are also human beings... often emotionally attached to the history of their own people". After eighteen centuries, he and his team would walk to the excavation sites "through the ruins of a Roman camp" whose troops had "caused the death of our forefathers. Nothing remains here today of the Romans save a heap of stones on the face of the desert, but here the descendants of the besieged were returning to salvage their ancestors' precious belongings".

One of Babata's documents, papyrus 12, addressed to the two guardians of her orphaned son

The Babata letters before opening

Masada

The next major discovery of ancient writings in Israel was made four years later, and they, like the manuscripts from the Bar Kochba caves, also have an honoured place in the Shrine of the Book. The scene of the find was again the Dead Sea area, and the occasion was the dramatic two-season archaeological excavation undertaken by Yigael Yadin between 1963 and 1964 on the summit of Masada, the immense rock that rises above the western shore some twenty-five miles due south of Qumran. King Herod turned the top of this rock into a formidable fortress in the latter half of the first century B.C.E. In 73 C.E., it became the grim scene of the last stand by the Jewish Zealots against the power of Rome.

Unlike the Bar Kochba exploration, which had the specific aim of searching for scrolls, Yadin's purpose was to carry out a systematic and comprehensive excavation of Masada, and penetrate the secrets of its history through the ruins of its structures and artefacts. He hoped, of course, that he might also be rewarded with the discovery of a body of writing, but it would be satisfaction enough if he succeeded in unearthing sufficient material remains to make possible a reconstruction of the story of the site.

He succeeded in both, and the finds in both categories were exciting. The scholar's spade turned up the ruins of lavish Herodian palaces, a casemate wall running round the perimeter of the summit, towers, pools and Roman-type bath-houses, a synagogue, an ingenious water system, and — in stark contrast to the handsome structures built nearly a hundred years earlier by luxury-loving Herod — the makeshift improvisations of the embattled Zealots who were the last Jewish resistance fighters to hold out against the Romans after the fall of Jerusalem in 70 C.E. Masada fell three years later under gruesome circumstances, and Yadin unearthed evidence of the Zealots' final hour.

He also found their writings, parts of the sacred biblical books which had fortified their spirits throughout adversity, and which they had hidden before taking their lives when the situation became hopeless. Portions of no fewer than fourteen scrolls were discovered. This was spectacular for, up to then, parchment manuscripts had withstood complete disintegration in the hot and dry Dead Sea

Masada at the time of the excavations

region — but only in caves. Now, at Masada, for the first time in archaeological history they were discovered among ruined buildings. Moreover, they were found in an archaeological stratum which could be dated with accuracy as not later than 73 C.E. — though they may have been written much earlier.

Parts of two scrolls had been hidden beneath the floor of a chamber which the Zealots had converted into a synagogue. A third was retrieved from the rubble behind Herod's northern palace-villa. A fourth scroll was unearthed in a tower in the casemate wall after a nine-foot mound of debris had been removed. The remaining ten were found in chambers in that wall.

Most of the scrolls were biblical. One contained parts of the Book of Ezekiel, another of Deuteronomy, two bore several chapters of Leviticus, two others chapters of the Book of Psalms. Their texts are almost identical with the Hebrew biblical texts in current use: the differences are very minor. The Psalms recited in today's synagogues are the same as those chanted by the Zealots in their summit synagogue — the same Hebrew words, the same sentence structure, the same beginning and end of each verse and paragraph.

One of the non-biblical texts was sectarian. This was The Songs of the Sabbath Sacrifices, which most probably originated with the Qumran sect. Though they had broken with the Jewish religious authorities in the land, some of them had taken part in the Jewish revolt against the Romans, and a few — in the opinion of Yadin — probably joined the Zealots at Masada to continue the resistance after the fall of Jerusalem, and would have taken their sacred scrolls with them.

The most important of the non-biblical scrolls, however, were two works which are well known in translation but whose original Hebrew composition had long vanished. Both contained the original Hebrew texts: one turned out to be a portion of the Book of Jubilees, a book in the Pseudepigrapha, written in the latter part of the second century B.C.E. The other and more important scroll, and the only one that was complete, was The Wisdom of Ben Sira, a book in the Apocrypha also known as Ecclesiasticus (not to be confused with the biblical Book of Ecclesiastes), written by Joshua Ben Sira at the beginning of the second century B.C.E.

Fragment of a Psalms scroll, Chaps. 82–85, found at Masada

לעולם   וישלחו מ...
            ...ישמ...ך

            מוב לאסף
...חיים נינבעו... אל
...רו...ם תעזבטו של...
...נו ורע חמר...
מיך וישים...ם היעלו
דישכנה ענחדלו
אנו יערתי צלאים אתם
יונבעים תעדחו
קוזכ...אלהם...סאר...אים

שרי לבכו... ל...סף   יל...ם...שלהש ל...
אלה...אים... וא...ש...
...
הברו לא...נ...
ט... ...ש דבי...
...ים וא...וע...
...נ...
...אב והחיים   ...
...ם   גם אשור נלוה יעמ...
עשוה לאם נברק ...סורא
נ...ר...בע... ...אר   קנש...
...ר...יע...מ... נ...רב...ראב
...ש...ך... ... ...נמר   אשר אל...יע...שא...
                אלהים שי...מ...אל
                מק... לפני...וח
מ...רכ...כס ערך   ...לא...מ...ל...ח... ...ם
פל...א עלאהם קלו   ...ס...טך תב...לם

Neither of these two works was included in the Hebrew canon, and they ceased to appear in Hebrew. The texts, in their original tongue, had now been recovered at Masada. The Book of Jubilees is an expanded narration of Genesis and the first fourteen chapters of Exodus, together with a commentary. It belongs to a group of visionary books 'falsely attributed' to the ancient prophets and accordingly called the Pseudepigrapha. Only some of the Eastern Churches hold a few of these books sacred. They are, however, of literary and historical interest to scholars.

The Apocrypha, on the other hand, was incorporated in the canon of the Roman Catholic and the Greek Orthodox churches, and the Wisdom of Ben Sira is among its most distinguished works. It is also the only apocryphal book which was highly esteemed by the rabbinical sages, despite its exclusion from the Hebrew Scriptures, and is frequently quoted in the Talmud. It is in the literary tradition of old Hebrew wisdom, and reflects the influence on Ben Sira of the biblical Book of Proverbs. It sings the praises of the righteous men of Israel, and presents wisdom as a revelation of the Lord and a guide to human conduct. Its moral themes are presented in the form of proverbs

These, then, are the treasures of history now accessible to all in Jerusalem's Shrine of the Book. Even for the layman, seeing these writings — direct communications from the ancient world to the present — is a moving encounter. For the Hebrew-speaking Israeli, able to recognize, read and follow the ancient Hebrew text, there is an added dimension of excitement and significance. To the scholar, it is an amazing boon, clearing wide paths towards the enlargement of knowledge and understanding in all academic disciplines related to the world of the Bible. The search for scrolls continues, discovery having sharpened the prospects for further finds. Those already brought to light, and on display in the Shrine of the Book, hold enough clues to the past to keep scholars occupied for centuries to come.

Selected Bibliography

Black, M. *The Scrolls and Christian Origins: Studies in the Jewish Background of the New Testament*. London: Nelson, 1961; New York: Scribner, 1961; new ed. California: Scholars Press, 1983.

Burrows, M. *The Dead Sea Scrolls*. New York: Viking Press, 1955; London: Secker and Warburg, 1956; new ed. Michigan: Baker Books, 1978.

___. *More Light on the Dead Sea Scrolls*. London: Secker and Warburg, 1958; New York: Viking Press, 1958.

Cross, F. M., Jr. *The Ancient Library of Qumran and Modern Biblical Studies*. New York: Doubleday, 1958; London: Duckworth, 1961; rev. ed. Michigan: Baker Books, 1980.

Cross, F. M., Jr., and S. Talmon, eds. *Qumran and the History of the Biblical Text*. London: Harvard University Press, 1975; Massachusetts: Harvard University Press, 1976.

Dupont-Sommer, A. *The Jewish Sect of Qumran and the Essenes*. London: Vallentine Mitchell, 1954; New York: Macmillan, 1956.

Flusser, D. "The Dead Sea Sect and Pre-Pauline Christianity." *Scripta Hierosolymitana* IV (1958).

Horgan, M. P. *Pesharim: Qumran Interpretations of Biblical Books*. Washington, D.C.: Catholic Biblical Association, 1979.

Sanders, J. A. *The Dead Sea Psalms Scroll*. New York: Cornell University Press, 1967.

Stendahl, K., ed. *The Scrolls and the New Testament*. New York: Harper, 1957; London: SCM Press, 1958; new ed. Connecticut: Greenwood Press, 1975. Vaux, R. de. *Archaeology and the Dead Sea Scrolls*. Schweich Lectures. Oxford/New York: OUP for the British Academy, 1973.

Vermes, G. *The Dead Sea Scrolls*. London: Penguin, Third Edition, 1987.

Yadin, Y., ed. *The Scroll of the War of the Sons of Light Against the Sons of Darkness*. Oxford: OUP, 1962.

___. *Tefillin from Qumran*. Jerusalem: The Israel Exploration Society and the Shrine of the Book, 1969.

___. *Bar Kokhba*. London: Weidenfeld and Nicolson, 1971; Jerusalem: Weidenfeld and Nicolson, 1971.

___. *The Temple Scroll*. London: Weidenfeld und Nicolson, 1985.

Woolen cloth from the Cave of Letters